THE ISRAEL LOBBY ENTERS STATE GOVERNMENT

RISE OF THE VIRGINIA ISRAEL ADVISORY BOARD

GRANT F. SMITH

Copyright © 2019 Institute for Research: Middle Eastern Policy, Inc.
All rights reserved.
Library of Congress Cataloging-in-Publication Data
Names: Smith, Grant F., author.
Title: The Israel Lobby Enters State Government – Rise of the
Virginia Israel Advisory Board / Grant F. Smith.
Description: Washington, D.C.: Institute for Research: Middle
Eastern Policy, Inc., [2019] | Includes bibliographical references.
Identifiers: LCCN 2019916646 (print) | LCCN 2019916646 (eBook)
| ISBN 9780982775738

The author wishes to thank the Virginia Coalition for Human Rights for their relentless pursuit of truth, transparency, justice and accountability across Virginia.

CONTENTS

EXHIBITS

INTRODUCTION

*We're a state agency that is funded by the state, with a core mandate of bringing Israeli companies to Virginia. [1] **VIAB Executive Director Dov Hoch addressing a 2019 Jewish Community Relations Council event.***

Across America, state governments are becoming ever more intensely involved in crafting and passing laws designed to advance the interests of a foreign government. Resolutions affirming Israel's "right to defend itself." Executive orders, resolutions and laws outlawing or condemning the Boycott, Divestment and Sanctions (BDS) movement. Budget line items for government officials to embark on continual trade development missions to Israel.

Ask any legislator why and you'll likely get an "intrinsic good" explanation. Advancing Israel is a vital U.S. national interest. So, shoveling hundreds of millions more Israel's way from state coffers is also just the right thing to do.

At the federal level, Israel already receives more U.S. foreign (mostly military) aid, secret intelligence, loan guarantees, favorable taxation and diplomatic support than any foreign country. The explanations for this are similarly broad. "Israel is a vital ally of the United States." First in the Cold War standoff with the Soviet Union. Now in the ongoing "War on Terror," they say.

Yet in reality, federal support for Israel is more convincingly explained as the result of a vast network of coordinated political campaign contributions, propaganda and coercion many Americans now refer to simply as the "Israel lobby." In my 2016 book, "Big Israel: How Israel's Lobby Moves America," I outlined how Zionism swept through establishment Jewish organizations from the late 19th century until support for Israel became the default stance of the "Israel advocacy ecosystem."

With the support of foreign guidance[2] and startup funding, the lead lobbying organization today known as the American Israel Public Affairs Committee (AIPAC) sits atop a $6 billion Israel affinity network that

---

[1] Dov Hoch, "What VIAB Does and How It Benefits Virginia," speech at the Weinstein Jewish Community Center, Richmond, VA, April 4, 2019. Introduction and remarks by former president of the Jewish Federation of Richmond Nathan Shor

[2] A frank telling of David Ben Gurion's efforts to set up a lobby and arms smuggling network in the U.S. is told in the 2019 book by Dennis Ross and David Makovsky "Be Strong and of Good Courage."

heavily—and as we and others argue, negatively—influences nearly every issue in Congress. AIPAC's influence as a foreign interest lobby was made possible by the defeat of Kennedy administration Department of Justice and Senate Foreign Relations Committee investigations which I detailed my 2008 book "America's Defense Line: The Justice Department's Battle to Register the Israel Lobby as Agents of a Foreign Government." As the book reveals, the world today would be very different if the laws of the land had been faithfully upheld in the 1960s. Instead, despite close ongoing coordination with Israel's government, the Israel advocacy ecosystem is allowed to skirt the Foreign Agents Registration Act.

In *Big Israel*, I looked at how news reporting and media outlets critical of the pervasive "pro-Israel" stance of government and politicians are shut down by Israel lobby watchdog organizations. I explored how laws designed to protect the U.S. from foreign espionage, lobbying and meddling in elections have largely been transcended by the Israel affinity ecosystem. Politicians in every congressional and presidential race vie to "out-Israel" their rivals since no other option is possible in the current system. Russian and other state actor meddling in America pales in comparison to Israel's.

The dominance of the Israel lobby leads to both catastrophic and merely highly negative outcomes for the United States. The most recent catastrophe is certainly the U.S. invasion of Iraq, which Israel lobbying organizations such as AIPAC lobbied for intensely, while simultaneously denying any role.[3]

But less costly and less visible examples abound. America's worst bilateral trade deal was signed with Israel as I detailed in the 2009 book "Spy Trade: How Israel's Lobby Undermines America's Economy." Even in 2019, by cumulative, inflation adjusted trade deficit, it is still the worst bilateral free trade agreement.[4] Ongoing pressure to maintain U.S. troops the Middle East, and in particular Iraq and Syria. The creation of an entirely new division of the U.S. Department of Treasury—the Office of Terrorism and Financial Intelligence (OTFI)—to promote Israeli interests through U.S. economic warfare which hurt the U.S. and global economy while ignoring Israeli support for arms trafficking, smuggling, corruption, illegal settlement finance and nuclear proliferation.

Is such a corrupt system entirely unbeatable? Of course not. During the Obama administration's negotiations to pass the Iran nuclear deal,

---

[3] See Mearsheimer, John and Walt, Stephen, 2008, "The Israel Lobby and U.S. Foreign Policy" New York, Farrar, Straus and Giroux

[4] See the report, "U.S. Israel Free Trade Agreement Damage Assessment." IRmep, June 20, 2019, https://IRmep.org/06202019_ILFTA.html

major establishment Israel affinity organizations[5] lobbied intensely to oppose passage of the agreement. Their propaganda organs, such as the *Weekly Standard* published endless diatribes to turn Americans against the deal. The Israeli government even spied on negotiations and leaked damaging information to allies in the U.S.

In the midst of the fight, IRmep (the nonprofit organization I founded and run) obtained tightly held U.S. government information about Israel's nuclear weapons production infrastructure, including hydrogen bomb development. American government officials never talk about Israel's nuclear weapons, and it took an expensive courtroom brawl for IRmep to obtain the Israeli file through the Freedom of Information Act.

The news media mostly shies away from reporting about Israel's nukes, eager not to jeopardize dwindling advertising revenues. But they couldn't ignore IRmep's release of the damning U.S. Department of Defense report "Critical Technology Assessment in Israel and NATO Nations."[6]

The *Weekly Standard* was the most upset. Long accustomed to having almost unchallenged authority to indicate the proper way forward for Middle East policy, the *Weekly Standard* accused the Obama administration of intentionally leaking the report to undermine Israeli opposition to the Joint Comprehensive Plan of Action or JCPOA.

In the end, the JCPOA was implemented, temporarily averting a U.S. war with Iran that Israel and many within the Israel affinity ecosystem were encouraging the Obama administration to launch. Later, the *Weekly Standard* folded, while IRmep continues.

I believe that exposure by IRmep of uncomfortable facts helped propel forward a deal that averted a war long promoted by the Israel lobby. IRmep continues to issue such facts, including accurate representative

---

[5] Not-for-profit Israel Affinity Organizations (IAOs) are entities that prioritize support Israel in both common and unique ways. Together, they make up the Israel lobby. Even the smallest organizations engage in multiple tactics, from taking influential Americans on trips to Israel, reactive media pressure campaigns, hosting on-campus Israel advocacy programs, publishing advocacy literature and academic studies, to proactively placing editorials and op-eds in elite and hometown newspapers. They convene non-stop conferences and events aimed at shaping U.S. foreign policy. They also groom and advance advocates for service as political appointees in government. For a thorough examination see the author's 2016 book "Big Israel: How Israel's Lobby Moves America," Washington, DC, Institute for Research, Middle Eastern Policy, Inc"

[6] To review briefs filed in the FOIA lawsuit and the report on Israel's nuclear weapons production facilities, see, https://IRmep.org/CFP/DoD/

polls revealing that Americans aren't quite so enamored of Israel or its lobby's demands as the Israel affinity ecosystem says they are.

But, as is often the case, the Israel lobby inserted a poison pill into the JCPOA. It had to be renewed and signed off by the president every six months. The lobby had already inserted another such poison pill in the 1995 Jerusalem Embassy Act, which mandated that the U.S. had to violate international law by moving its embassy to the contested city of Jerusalem. Up until 2017 Presidents faithfully signed waivers, citing U.S. national interests in not moving. But eventually, as the Israel lobby well knew, a president would arrive on the scene who would disregard U.S. interests and do its bidding.

That president is Donald J. Trump. Not only did he move the U.S. embassy from Tel Aviv to Jerusalem, he scuttled the JCPOA. In doing so, Trump and the lobby have moved the U.S. a bit closer to yet another unnecessary war that could prove disastrous not only for the people of the region and United States, but the entire world.

On the bright side, there is growing debate taking place about the Israel lobby and much more popular awareness of its disastrous programs. The growth of social media and high quality alternative news outlets has helped. There is now even an annual conference at the National Press Club which, for seven years running, that makes a damage assessment and proposes actionable alternatives. The conference is nonpartisan and features a wide range of voices.[7]

And it is from this conference this small attempt to shine light on the harmful work of the Israel affinity ecosystem began. In 2019 in the final conference panel and at the end of the day, the Virginia Coalition for Human Rights made a stunning revelation. In the Commonwealth, local Jewish federations helped create, move to the legislature and now controlled an agency within state government called the Virginia Israel Advisory Board. VIAB uses state funding to raise the inflow of Israeli exports, launch Israeli companies (often in direct competition with innovative Virginia companies), and enrich its members. The federations are attempting to insert Israeli government propaganda into the curriculum in the K-12 system.

As is generally the case nationally, mainstream news organizations such as the *Richmond-Times-Dispatch* and local television networks report little to nothing about VIAB except what look like recycled news releases of its job creation claims. Like AIPAC, VIAB is extremely secretive, even giving code-names to its initiatives to avoid scrutiny.

However, unlike the American Israel Public Affairs Committee, which considers secrecy essential to its success, VIAB has a large Achilles heel—

---

[7] The publisher of this book is an official conference co-organizer.

the Virginia Freedom of Information Act. While AIPAC can lobby endlessly for disastrous policies like the Iraq invasion confident that the story won't emerge until years later, and then only anecdotally—VIAB cannot. State agencies in Virginia respect and rigorously uphold the Virginia Freedom of Information Act. Unlike the federal Freedom of Information Act, the state VFOIA requires a response in only five, as opposed to 20 days. This makes collecting information about VIAB a relatively efficient effort.

Older, more established nodes of the Israel lobby are sometimes alarmed by VIAB's audacity. In the midst of a 2018 VIAB driven reconstitution to relieve itself of oversight by the Office of the Governor (and slip the bonds of travel expense reimbursement rules), the Jewish Community Relations Council of Greater Washington warned, "the request to grant Virginia's Israel development activities special status, status that no other economic development group enjoys, may draw negative attention to VIAB and result in VIAB's dissolution and absorption into Virginia's greater economic development activities."

For outsiders, the warning requires translation. VIAB's right to secretly pursue Israeli economic interests in Virginia could have been diluted if not destroyed by forcing it to merge with the Virginia Economic Development Partnership. VEDP works for the interests of residents of the entire state. It doesn't secretly advance foreign country interests, and generally avoids duplication of effort. In short, stripping away all of the inherent characteristics that make VIAB a negative influence in Virginia would destroy it. There is no simple way to make VIAB serve the broader interests of Virginia, since its function is to increase Israel's exports and enrich and empower the state Israel advocacy ecosystem.

But VIAB pressed ahead with a reconstitution despite the warning, revealing its true power.

The larger question is whether VIAB represents a new and dangerous stage of the Israel lobby's spread throughout America. There are many front groups masquerading as not-for-profit chambers of commerce constantly pushing state and region-wide governments to act in Israel's interest. But—so far—none have leveraged their power to create a new state agency. VIAB's new executive director, Dov Hoch, provides testimony that outside chambers of commerce simply cannot score the big wins a government agency like VIAB can.

The stakes are high. The Israel lobby wants to place limits on Americans' right to free speech about the Israel Palestine situation. They want to entwine Israeli business interests deeply into every major economic activity of interest to Israeli corporations that they cannot be undone. They seek undue influence to tap vast, deep pools of funding within many states that are mostly unprotected from the onslaught. They wish to make state governments as compliant and obedient to their demands—however harmful—as members of Congress and the U.S. president now are to AIPAC demands.

Since VIAB is the vanguard of this damaging new development, I am focusing specifically on its operations in Virginia with a particular focus on new businesses. Using sources made available through VFOIA, including internal emails, grant and loan applications to major Virginia development funds, and legislative records, I have uncovered a pattern of self-dealing, corruption and foreign influence.

Revelation of these damning facts—if they become broadly known—could overturn the Israel lobby's current drive to harness Virginia in service to Israel's interests through control of a state agency. However, like the JCPOA, any victory would be only temporary. Another VIAB would be sure to pop up—mostly under the radar—in some other state or regional entity. The entities that created and provide board members to VIAB, have been active for decades and have access to vast and stable funding. So, this book explores with none of the usual qualifications, the interconnectivity between the Jewish establishment, Israel, campaign contributions and compares it with other state groups.

One reason this book even came into being is secrecy. Secrecy is the enemy of accountability and good governance. Government and business circles in the United States are rife with operatives and entities that cloak their activities and true motives in cascading veils of secrecy.

In the post-911 era, federal government secrecy has reached freakish new heights. Not only will federal government agencies generally refuse to search for responsive information sought under Freedom of Information Act. The Department of Justice, responding to one of my lawsuits, has told a judge, without batting an eyelid, that covering up illegal government wrongdoing via secrecy is permissible, legal and even justifiable.[8]

Government and for-profit corporations also hold the common belief than even the most mundane interaction amongst them automatically can generate exclusion from the public record as an interchange of trade secrets, which is therefore a defensible reason for withholding of information. This is not only operative at federal levels, but embedded in many state sunshine laws as well.

It therefore came as no particular surprise that Mel Chaskin, longtime Chairman of the Virginia Israel Advisory Board, refused to respond to my

---

[8] See an IRmep lawsuit to compel the release of presidential memos promising not to enforce the Arms Export Control Act in response to Israel's nuclear weapons program on the IRmep website at:
https://IRmep.org/CFP/letters/default.asp

requests for information under the Virginia Freedom of Information Act (VFOIA).

VIAB represented an irresistible subject for a VFOIA inquiry. Unlike, the American Israel Public Affairs Committee, VIAB as a state agency is legally bound to respond to requests for documents. AIPAC's secrecy is legendary. It doesn't have to explain why it maintains an office in Israel or what ongoing coordination occurs between its lobbyists and Israeli government officials. But, theoretically anyway, if VIAB held a meeting with Israeli government officials, it would have to disclose minutes of the meeting.

In theory anyway.

As VIAB churned out report after report claiming stunning job creation and tax revenues from its Virginia projects, it seemed sensible to ask VIAB for the source of their claims. There was good reason to do so.

Before stepping down at the end of the McAuliffe administration in January of 2018, Virginia Secretary of Commerce Todd Patterson Haymore complained in a private email to other members of the governor's office about VIAB's job creation claims. "I can't argue with the short annual report where they stated they helped create 127 jobs/$436k tax dollars; however, the annual report is likely the most inflated without merit that I've seen in my decade here."

Was VIAB simply pulling numbers out of the air? Or was there a sophisticated econometric model populated with real data and input from state tax and employment agencies driving their claims? On May 2, 2019 I sent Mel Chaskin, and Dov Hoch, VIAB's new executive director, a VFOIA request for "a copy of the econometric model substantiating VIAB's quantitative public claims of jobs created, ROI and tax revenue generated for the Commonwealth of Virginia in 2018."[9]

At the time VIAB didn't have, as it was supposed to, any contact for VFOIA requests listed on its website. But Chaskin was game and dubbed himself VIAB's "FOIA disclosure officer" in his May 9, 2019 response.

At first, he was a bit testy, warning that any response was only warranted for "citizens of the Commonwealth of Virginia, representatives of newspaper and magazines with circulation in the Commonwealth and representatives of radio and television stations broadcasting in or into the Commonwealth." Then Chaskin, eased up a bit,

---

[9] VIAB claimed it had, "contributed to creating 177 new jobs last year, many in established companies that will continue to add jobs next year." VIAB also claimed, "Israeli companies' tax contribution to the Virginia Treasury exceeded 25 times VIAB's budget in 2018, rendering a 550% ROI over the terms of the past four Governors." Source Virginia Israel Advisory Board Annual Report FY 2018, page 3.

Even assuming, arguendo, [yes, he actually put that in italics] you were a citizen of the Commonwealth, please be advised that the Virginia Freedom of Information Act governs public access to information contained in existing documents. FOIA imposes no obligation on a public body to conduct legal or other research or to answer questions unrelated to or unsubstantiated by existing documentation or records maintained by that public body, nor does it require a public body to create a record if a record does not already exist. The VIAB has no existing documents responsive to your request.

So, VIAB's chairman wasn't going to substantiate VIAB's economic claims. I decided to ask another tantalizing question about VIAB that went to the heart of its secrecy—the Israeli companies behind its many code-named projects.

Code named Israeli projects were irresistible targets, because they smacked of international clandestine operations. I once unexpectedly received a trove FBI documents via FOIA in 2012 linking Hollywood movie producer Arnon Milchan, convicted felon Richard Kelly Smyth, and Israeli Prime Minister Benjamin Netanyahu, to a smuggling ring that illegally spirited hundreds of nuclear weapons triggers out of the U.S.[10] The most surprising gem within the release was not that the FBI had read up on "Who's Who in America" before deciding to steer entirely clear of Milchan. It also wasn't that the U.S. news media never subsequently did a single story on Netanyahu's personal involvement. That is not an unusual state of affairs in the mainstream media. I learned long ago that's just not their beat. The amazing thing in the release of the formerly classified documents was the code name the international smuggling trio gave to their smuggling ring. Project Pinto!

For those too young to remember, the Ford Pinto was a subcompact car sold by Ford Motor Company between 1971 and 1980. They were stubby, under powered and innocuous. But if unexpectedly rear-ended, given its faulty fuel-tank design, the Pinto could explode into a ball of flame. Was Project Pinto an upgrade to Israel's nuclear weapons that would automatically generate balls of fire if, say, the country was again surprised by unexpected military attack?

Krytrons are innocuous and hard to distinguish from harmless consumer electronic components. When Richard Kelly Smyth began shipping krytrons from Huntington Beach-based MILCO International

---

[10] See Grant F. Smith "How to Smuggle U.S. Nuclear Triggers to Israel – New DHS files raise questions about Arnon Milchan" Antiwar.com, May 11, 2017. https://original.antiwar.com/smith-grant/2017/05/10/how-to-smuggle-us-nuclear-triggers-to-israel/

on January 7, 1980 through the ring to their ultimate destination, the Israeli Ministry of Defense, he falsely claimed on export documentation that they were common vacuum tube "pentodes." Krytrons, like pentodes, are also glass vacuum tubes. But wire together two, four, or more and you have the precisely timed detonating circuits needed to touch off a nuclear device. Project Pinto. Devilish brilliance!

But unlike the krytron smuggling network, VIAB was churning out code names in practically every other board meeting, all the while swearing attendees to secrecy. Project Turbine. Ballistic. Project Re-Cycle. Salty Fish Sea. Ecowave Power. Vegan Non-Meat producer and Packager. And the biggest, most secret of them all, "Project Jonah." What was Jonah all about? As it turns out, it was about an Israeli company, AquaMaof, taking over the market share of an innovative, socially conscious homegrown Virginia producer. Project Jonah reveals just how much harm a rogue, secretive Israel export promotion board masquerading as a Virginia state agency can actually do.

However, it was necessary to dig deeper than VIAB's already public board meeting minutes. That is because whenever an Israeli company name was about to pop out of obscurity, Chaskin , or some other board member quickly swept the room into a "closed session" that would not be documented in publicly releasable meeting minutes. VIAB is highly aware of, and seems opposed to, the Virginia Freedom of Information Act.

Nevertheless, on May 20, 2019 I sent Chaskin another VFOIA request. This time I included my press pass as a representative of the venerable *Washington Report on Middle East Affairs,* which publishes some of my reports. The pass was issued by its late founder Andy Kilgore. Chaskin's second response was, if possible, even less friendly than his first.

> *Please be advised that, pursuant to Virginia Code Section 2.2-3705.6(3), public records containing [P]roprietary information, voluntarily provided by private business pursuant to a promise of confidentiality from a public body, used by the public body for business, trade, and tourism development or retention; and memoranda, working papers, or other information related to businesses that are considering locating or expanding in Virginia, prepared by a public body, where competition or bargaining is involved and where disclosure of such information would adversely affect the financial interest of the public body are excluded from the mandatory disclosure provisions of FOIA. The records you seek contain propriety information provided by private businesses to the VIAB pursuant to a promise of confidentiality and are used by the VIAB for business, trade, and tourism development and*

retention. As such, the requested records are exempt from the mandatory disclosure provisions of FOIA and will not be produced.

It was then and there that I decided four things. The first was not to ask VIAB for any more information about its operations in Virginia. After two attempts it seemed like an entirely fruitless endeavor.

The second was to publicly unmask as many Israeli companies behind VIAB's code-named projects as possible. This book is the result. It was first intended to be a lengthy but manageable article for the *Washington Report on Middle East Affairs.* But after a trip through Virginia, starting in Richmond, and close to 50 VFOIAs, the information quickly grew to book length as tantalizing information flooded in from multiple non-VIAB sources.

The third was realization that VIAB was probably not code-naming Israeli military contractors in its materials. Mel Chaskin is a Northern Virginia military contractor who has done extremely well for himself. Israeli military contractors are clearly a large part of the VIAB equation due to a "buy American" clauses in the latest 10-year foreign aid package to Israel. I therefore cover the uncomfortable background in a chapter that doesn't do very much unmasking, since the masks were never laid on VIAB's board room table.

However, one VIAB-backed project is publicly known. Oran Safety Glass, a military contractor that originated on a small Israeli kibbutz, has been a VIAB flagship. What has recently become public is that OSG's military contracting fraud has endangered the massive state funds that have been invested in its formation and expansion in Emporia.

The fourth finding is that some code names are merely "multiple bites of the same apple." That is to say, an Israeli company such as OSG that came in at VIAB's invitation and hoovered up huge amounts of state resources and political capital from the Commonwealth. Liking how it tasted, the beneficial owners of the Israeli operations then circled back for more.

Fifth, I have added Sabra Dipping Company. Sabra charged into Virginia, scooped up state funds and has nearly wiped out the market share of a sympathetic, even symbolic American competitor in New England. But Sabra didn't ever really need a code name. Rather, with large backers behind it such Israel's Strauss Group and later PepsiCo, Sabra appeared to be able to pursue the traditional route of large Virginia entrants such as Amazon. Sabra ruthlessly pitted political jurisdictions against one another. It seized and toyed with them and squeezed them until the right mix of free money, tax holidays, and other concessions dribbled out of Sabra's industrial-sized lemon juice extractor in sufficient quantities. So, Sabra may never have really needed VIAB's "services" for market entry.

But VIAB needs Sabra's services. It merely has to gesture toward Sabra's massive Colonial Heights plant to make all of its blue-sky, secret projects bearing highly unlikely economic development forecasts seem plausible enough to gobble up more state resources and attention. One VIAB board member has even used a list of such secret projects to obtain relief on $210,000 he personally owed on a failed project. And the free money grabs have been so fast and furious that even Sabra's holding company CEO wants in on smaller, high risk VIAB projects. Sabra itself is circling back for more state subsidies and VIAB is on record supporting those. So, I included a chapter on Sabra Dipping Company.

In retrospect, VIAB clearly didn't invest very much effort in some of its code names. This is a bit of a letdown, but understandable. Israel is a small place. How many wave-powered energy generation companies can it have? Not many it turns out. Therefore, I wrote a chapter on Ecowave Power, the code name for Ecowave Power Ltd. Its unsatisfyingly short code name was unnecessarily revealing. As a public service to readers and listeners, I've deleted the chapter. But VIAB did try very hard to keep secret the Israeli companies behind other code named projects. The reasons only became clear after months of digging. It had nothing to do with the reasons Mel Chaskin wrote in his VFOIA response.

Some of the Israeli companies either now in or desperately trying to get into Virginia are doing business in illegal settlements or on lands unlawfully seized through warfare, or illegally seized from Palestinians, Druze and Syrians. However, even when a VIAB project leaves the secret startup phase and begins selling products and services, the secret shell company that shields ultimate beneficial owners in Israel seems like a giveaway.

That is the story of Sun Tribe Solar.

Some code name startups are teetering on the edge of bankruptcy in Israel, have no real comparative advantages or defensible patents, or are obviously stultifying unprepared to compete on a level playing field in Virginia or anywhere else in the United States.

Others have a value proposition or business model that seems just plain unviable, such as UBQ. UBQ will only survive if the entire public perception of the real issues in waste management are overturned in a flood of unjustifiable state funding.

Some reasons for VIABs secrecy were much closer to home. VIAB wanted to leverage long term relationships with local gatekeepers in order to tap huge vaults of taxpayer and other cash unique to Virginia. VIAB board members and contractors wanted to have a foot simultaneously on both sides of a deal, shepherding the project along from inside VIAB, while simultaneously occupying positions as equity stakeholders on corporate boards of directors of the U.S. subsidiaries of the very Israeli companies they were bringing into Virginia. In simpler words, board members at VIAB are engaged in blatant self-dealing.

That combined with VIAB's uncanny access to local market intelligence, fellow Virginia state agencies, the governor's office, legislature and capital, leverage these synergies into state-funding propelled comparative advantages that enable Israeli partner and VIAB board members to seize market share from Virginia-grown and American-grown companies.

This is cronyism, Teapot Dome recast with southern hospitality and charm.

VIAB's attempted state-level economic and political takeovers also resemble AIPAC's takeover of Congress, which though opposed by an array of seemingly unbeatable forces, ultimately prevailed. Back in the 1960s and 70s few watchdogs even perceived what was happening. Fewer still alerted the public. As Israel affinity groups in other states ponder whether to reconstitute their local groups into a VIAB-like government configurations, Americans who prefer to keep foreign export promotion boards and state government separate, their textbooks propaganda free, and their free speech rights intact—had better carefully consider the lessons that can be learned from this book for their own home state.

1.

PROJECT BIODIESEL – THE JERUSALEM CONNECTION AND THE TOBACCO COMMISSION

Chuck Lessin briefed us on an Israeli project involving a new Israeli technology to develop biodiesel cost effectively and thus overcome the historical dependence on government subsidies that have plagued the industry. Chuck reported that because of his personal involvement with the project and its VIAB origin, he turned to Don Ferguson to clarify if there are any conflicts of interest and was told that there are no conflicts. **VIAB Board Meeting Minutes**[11]

George Packer's 2013 book *The Unwinding: An Inner History of the New America* chronicles North Carolina gas station, roadhouse restaurant and convenience store entrepreneur Dean Price. In the 1990s Price witnessed regional decline reflected in three key industries—furniture making, textiles and tobacco. After the 2005 landfall of Hurricane Katrina and other factors led to a doubling of diesel fuel prices, Ray Price fell in love with the idea of biodiesel. Partially driven by his intense dislike of foreign oil producers, Price believed he could make money and help local farmers transcend the coming apocalypse of "Peak Oil."

Peak oil is a forecast period in time when the maximum extraction of petroleum is reached, after which it enters into inevitable decline. M. King Hubbert, who coined the term, in 1956 theorized that peak oil production would occur in the year 2000, hitting 12.5 billion barrels per year. But subsequent theorists moved the date further into the future, while increasing the theoretical production capacity in line with ever evolving production data.

Armed with a powerful combination of theory, goodwill and desire to make a buck, Price founded a refinery sourcing locally grown canola into biodiesel. He had the significant advantage of control over distribution, since he sold the biodiesel through his chain of gasoline stations.

---

[11] VIAB board of directors meeting Minutes July 29, 2014

Dean Price was destroyed by his biodiesel venture. Despite his long experienced in the market, plummeting transportation fuel prices did him in.

POP'S BINGO WORLD AND THE JERUSALEM CONNECTION

Unlike Dean Price, Charles Lessin had no career in transportation fuels when he invested in a biodiesel startup in 2014. In his biography as vice chairman of the Virginia Israel Advisory Board, Lessin was touted as:

> *President and CEO of American Homecrafters Inc., based in Richmond, VA. American Homecrafters has developed and built over 300 exclusive single-family homes in the Richmond metropolitan area. Chuck continues to develop new and innovative business opportunities, including his latest venture Virginia On-Line Fantasy Sports, LLC.*[12]

Greater numbers of Virginians are more likely familiar with Lessin's other line of business, a bingo hall, which he operates on the fringes of the capital city of Richmond (population 227,000). Lessin's sprawling Pop's Bingo World has reported close to $40 million in revenue over the past two decades. That's why Lessin has been referred to as the "Bingo maven."[13] It all started as a small-time family business with no fixed location.

Patriarch Lenny Lessin and his sons Charles and Alan ran itinerant bingo games in the South Side of Richmond together for nearly fifteen years. In the early days, crowds of 150-200 would arrive at a local synagogue to play for a dollar per card, typically buying packs of 25 to 45 cards in cash. Over the course of an afternoon, winners of a round could net $100, or a daily jackpot of $1,000. A typical game required 30-40 calls to reach a winner.

Bingo can be traced back to a game of chance played in Italy in the early 1500s called "Il Giuoco del Lotto D'Italia" It's long been a successful money-raiser because of that same emotional "high" produced by any game of chance. Good customers tend to be repeat players, some spending down their Social Security check or other fixed income while enjoying an afternoon.

---

[12] Viab.org website consulted on September 2, 2019

[13] Simerman, John, July 21, 2010, "Richmond tries again with bingo hall", *East Bay Times*, https://www.eastbaytimes.com/2010/07/21/richmond-tries-again-with-bingo-hall/

For decades the only way to legally run bingo in Virginia has been on behalf of a nonprofit, charitable entity that runs the game with "volunteers." So, in 1984 the Lessins established and administered a non-profit called "The Jerusalem Connection." The Jerusalem Connection's stated mission at the time was clear—to prevent the intermarriage of Jews with non-Jews. Or, as it claimed on its non-profit tax return in 2000, to "help to combat the worldwide problem of assimilation."

At the time, anti-assimilation "education" was a major concern within establishment Jewish organizations in the United States. In 1998, Benjamin Netanyahu announced a new initiative directed against Jewish assimilation and intermarriage with non-Jews that he viewed as a "demographic threat." It was a jointly funded Israeli government–Jewish federations program called Birthright Israel. The program's free ten-day trips to Israel for teenage Jews from American colleges and universities have since been called "birthrate Israel" by some participants who saw that the transparent goal of the operation to get each traveler to marry one of his or her fellow Jews. The Jerusalem Connection duly provided funding to Birthright after its founding as well as to many other Jewish educational programs, mostly in the U.S., designed to keep Jews together and grounded through a religious education.

But Chuck Lessin was soon no longer running a synagogue basement operation. During the time of his transition to a full time bingo operation, only about 1.8percent of Virginia's population was Jewish, some 18,000 people with an estimated 12,500 living in and around Richmond.[14] He wanted to broaden the operation to reach a much more diverse mass market. But how would a more religious and ethnically diverse customer base feel about The Jerusalem Connection's core mission?

At first, Lessin didn't appear to worry much about that. In 2004 he launched a new purpose-built, 6,000 square foot bingo hall at 210 Giant Drive just off Midlothian Turnpike. It had a well-lit parking lot, modern bingo equipment, uniformed security guards and an affordable food menu so players didn't have to leave the facility. Since many bingo players like to smoke, he even spent $11,000 on an air filtration and extraction system. In honor of his father, who had passed away three years earlier, he dubbed it Pop's Bingo World.

---

[14] Virtual Jewish World: Virginia, United States, Jewish Virtual Library,
https://www.jewishvirtuallibrary.org/virginia-jewish-history

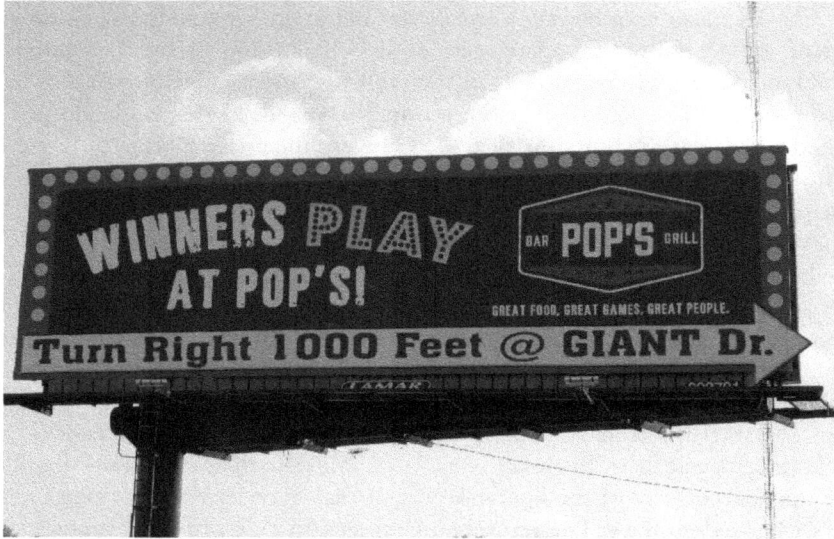

1 BILLBOARD ADVERTISING POP'S BINGO WORLD

It was an instant run-away success. Working with his father and brother in the late 1990's, Charles had struggled to break $100,000 per year in bingo revenues. In its first year of operations, Pop's Bingo World generated nearly $2 million in bingo revenues for The Jerusalem Connection.

But there was, of course, overhead. The Jerusalem Connection owned the buildings and had to make payments on the mortgage. Also, bingo players expect to win some rounds, and The Jerusalem Connection claimed it paid out $1.5 million in winnings. Still, the margins were good enough to make $47,000 in grants for "Jewish education" including to Birthright Israel.

Pop's Bingo World marched steadily along, usually producing 14 percent margins on annual bingo revenues, which climbed to $4 million in 2014 after a decade of operations. As part of the world of Jewish philanthropy, Lessin may have been monitoring the General Assembly of Jewish Federations as it began to soften its longstanding, hardline anti-assimilationist narrative. The reason for this softening was, as Michael Siegal, Chair of the Board of Trustees of Jewish Federations North America General Assembly (an umbrella organization to federations) said—somewhat like bingo itself. Being Jewish was now a numbers game:

Being Jewish is a numbers game. And some of the numbers should be keeping all of us up at night. Here are some numbers or you to think about. Six million Jews in North America, eight million Jews in the rest of the world. Fourteen million

> *people total. One fifth of one percent of the world's population.
> And now less than two percent of the North American
> population. Just on those numbers alone, we will be challenged
> as a community.*

So, the General Assembly began to take a much softer line on "anti-assimilation" rhetoric and emphasize "inclusiveness" to be able to count "mixed" Jewish non-Jewish families within Jewish federation "numbers."

Charles Lessin's The Jerusalem Connection, and it is fair to call it his, since Charles is the longest running board member, went with the flow. Lessin decided The Jerusalem Connection wasn't—publicly anyway—going to be anti-assimilationist anymore. ."

Late in 2011, The Jerusalem Connection told the IRS in a publicly available tax return filing that it was actually getting into the business of assimilation. Not by encouraging marriage between Jews and non-Jews. But rather:

> *The organization is using the services of rabbis, social workers
> and psychologists to reach out to those Americans temporarily
> living and studying Judaism in Israel, who require social service
> professionals to assist in the acclimatization process of Israeli
> life and culture. These Americans are in Israel to study Jewish
> law and bible in pursuit of becoming rabbis and teachers of
> Jewish studies. The main purpose is to provide emotional and
> spiritual support to these Americans who can't assimilate well
> in yeshivas and other institutions of learning in Israel.*[15]

Pop's made other moves that would lower potential public perceptions that it was an operation targeting the pocketbooks of mostly lower income non-Jews to subsidize mostly Jewish causes. In 2012 on the same property as the bingo hall, Pop's opened a community garden that grew vegetables to feed "200 needy people" and provided cut flowers to hospice care facilities. In 2010 Lessin also shifted business strategy by renting out Pop's hall to a local Boys and Girls Club to run the bingo rounds for a day with Pop's only sharing in the profits. Despite the strategy shift, net revenue at The Jerusalem Connection plunged, producing nearly $700,000 in losses between 2008 and 2014. Lessin had all the appearances of needing cash from another source.

---

[15] "The Jerusalem Connection," 2010 IRS form 990, statement of program service accomplishments.

CONFLICT OF INTEREST WAIVER FROM THE STATE ATTORNEY GENERAL

This apparently set Charles Lessin casting about for other opportunities. Lessin was a board member of the Virginia Israel Advisory Board under the office of the Governor. The board's work on a $1.5 million grant from the Tobacco Commission to VIAB's "Project Jonah" that began in the year 2013, explored later, must have made a big impression on Lessin.

Lessin formed Appalachian Biofuels LLC naming himself as its Chief Executive Officer. He briefed fellow VIAB board members in a July meeting that he was "personally involved" in:

> *...an Israeli project involving a new Israeli technology to develop biodiesel cost effectively and thus overcome the historical dependence on government subsidies that have plagued the industry.*

Donald Ferguson from the Office of Attorney General who attended the meeting, told the gathering he saw no conflicts of interest in such a deal.[16]

It was just five days before the VIAB meeting that Appalachian Biofuels, LLC had requested a $250,000 grant from the Tobacco Commission to develop the project through the Russell County Industrial Development Authority. Lessin told the Tobacco Commission that he'd also be soliciting $800,000 from the Virginia Coalfield Economic Development Authority, another grant of $300,000 for rail access to carry biodiesel fuel, and $355,000 in additional special projects funds from the Tobacco Commission. But what exactly is the Tobacco Commission?

VIAB AT THE TROF[17]

Virginia and other states settled lawsuits against major tobacco companies in 1998. The estimated revenue over the first 25 years of the settlement is $246 billion.[18] Unfortunately, most states spend less than

---

[16] VIAB board of directors meeting Minutes July 29, 2014

[17] Northam, Ralph S. Governor, Commonwealth of Virginia, December 18, 2018, "Executive Amendments to the 2018-2020 Budget" PDF page 19 https://dpb.virginia.gov/budget/buddoc19/BudgetDocument.pdf

[18] Tobacco Free Kids, "A State-by-State Look at the 1998 Tobacco Settlement 20 Years Later" https://www.tobaccofreekids.org/what-we-do/us/statereport

three percent of their settlement payouts on smoking cessation programs or preventing kids from smoking. These were the intended purpose of the damage settlement.

In Virginia, a portion of the tobacco settlement funding is distributed by a 28-member body created in 1999 now called the Tobacco Region Revitalization Commission. TRRC has awarded more than 2,000 grants totaling over a billion dollars across Virginia's tobacco region.[19]

The largest grants distributed by TRRC includes a $12 million grant to Liberty University Center for Medical and Health Sciences. In 2014 $10 million went to Virginia Electric & Power Company to build infrastructure in Brunswick County in the south of the commonwealth. In 2005 $8.1 million was paid out to Mid-Atlantic Broadband Communities Corporation for a regional telecommunications backbone initiative. Although the average grant paid out is less than half a million dollars, private companies, in partnership with county economic development agencies, sign performance agreements that obligate them to create a guaranteed number of jobs within a fixed time period as a condition for receiving grants. Those who are successful often return to the commission's Tobacco Region Opportunity Fund, or TROF, for multiple payouts.

The Tobacco Commission has been at the center of several scandals. Senator Phillip Puckett, a Democrat representing the 38th District of Virginia, was investigated by the FBI for a complex job swapping scheme. Puckett served on several legislative commissions and committees, including the Tobacco Commission.[20] In the midst of Governor Terry McAuliffe's 2014 drive to pass Medicare reform, Puckett suddenly announced his resignation from the Virginia Senate to assume a job at the GOP-controlled Tobacco Commission. This move torpedoed the Medicare legislation as control of the Senate shifted to Republicans. It also allowed Puckett's daughter to take a position she could not accept while her father was a state senator—Domestic & Juvenile Court judge.

Condemnations printed in the *Washington Post* thundered, "This is nothing short of bribery" and "The corrupt pay off the corrupt." Although

---

[19] The Tobacco Region Revitalization Commission is the new name for the Tobacco Indemnification and Community Revitalization Commission. The name was changed as part of an effort to reform how the commission operates. See Associated Press, May 15, 2015 "Lynchburg Native Feinman to lead Virginia tobacco commission."
https://www.newsadvance.com/news/local/lynchburg-native-feinman-to-lead-virginia-tobacco-commission/article_d0f15800-fb12-11e4-ba1f-57cee79afee4.html

[20] At the time it was still called the "Tobacco Indemnification & Community Revitalization Commission."

the FBI investigated and subpoenaed Tobacco Commission records, no criminal charges were ever filed. However, one FBI investigation into the Tobacco Commission that did lead to an embezzlement conviction was the case of the Literary Foundation of Virginia.

In 2001-2002 John W. Forbes served as Secretary of Finance of the Commonwealth of Virginia while also sitting on the board of the Tobacco Commission. Forbes sought a $5 million grant for a foundation to provide education to the residents in the Southside of Richmond and Southwest Virginia.

The Tobacco Commission wired $5 million in two installments to the Literary Society in 2002. But the organization had a sham board of directors. Forbes's wife served as Executive Director with a $130,000 per year salary. When Forbes left government in 2002, he assumed the job of Executive Director and siphoned out $4 million via other sham organizations that he then used for personal benefit. Forbes was sentenced to ten years in prison and ordered to pay $4 million in restitution to the Tobacco Commission.[21]

The Virginia Israel Advisory Board has successfully tapped the TROF many times to fund its Israel business projects. Because each grant requires a signed performance agreement, it is not supposed to simply be free money. For business startups, the performance agreements specify the number of jobs that must be created, average pay, and tax revenues generated. More recently, the performance agreements have become more demanding, requiring copies of tax return filings as proof that stated performance agreement metrics have been achieved. If a new startup fails, grantees are not supposed to keep the money instead of returning it as required by signed performance agreements. However, as discussed later, county monitoring of actual jobs and tax creation appears to be lax, and there is no real incentive to report that targets have not been met.

In the fall of 2019, the Virginia Tobacco Region Revitalization Commission office seemed to be keeping a low profile. It is not listed in the directory in the building where it is housed near the state capitol building. If you ask the reception desk why, they will helpfully explain that not all building offices are listed. But it may be found on the fifth floor in suite 503, behind a heavy secured wooded door with a brass nameplate.

In 2019 the executive director of the Tobacco Commission is Evan Feinman. Feinman's pathway to leadership of the commission was circuitous. When Terry McAuliffe was only a gubernatorial candidate,

---

[21] U.S. Attorney's Office, November 23, 2010, "Former Richmond Secretary of Finance Sentenced for Embezzling $4 million from Tobacco Indemnification Fund" https://archives.fbi.gov/archives/richmond/press-releases/2010/ri112310a.htm

Feinman worked in his campaign as policy director, frequently interacting with major donors on their policy requests.[22] After McAuliffe's victory, he appointed the then 31 year old Feinman to the position of Deputy Secretary of the Virginia's Department of Natural Resources. The agency had 2,400 employees and an annual budget of $420 million.[23]

Feinman is a lawyer from a family of lawyers. His father, Ron Feinman is the founder of One World Structured Settlements. A structured settlement takes a series of payments from a legal settlement, and for a fee, converts it into a lump sum payout for the recipient. Feinman the elder was past president of the Association of Fund Raising Professionals, and Regional Vice-Chair of the B'nai B'rith International Planned Giving Committee. B'nai B'rith, established in 1843, is one of the oldest Jewish organizations in the United States. It was originally created to help Jewish immigrants to the U.S. learn English and gain access to hospital care and life insurance. He was also a past board member of the University of Virginia Hillel Center. Hillels across the country actively promote Israel on American campuses, frequently targeting Palestinian student organizations and their actions and events spotlighting Israel's human rights abuses.

Evan Feinman's selection as head of the Tobacco Commission in May of 2015 was portrayed as part of Governor McAuliffe's attempt to make the commission more transparent and accountable after a comprehensive audit. Its name was changed from the "Tobacco Indemnification and Community Revitalization Commission" to the Tobacco Region Revitalization Commission. The renamed organization's turn-around was premised on no longer making grant awards based on political considerations. Transparency was to be achieved by creating an online database of awards.[24] The number of commission members was reduced to 28 from 31, while demonstrated experience in business, economic development, finance and education became a job requirement.[25]

Charles Lessin claimed that the private equity infusion portion into his biofuels deal would be $2.1 million, for a total $3.5 million project capital

---

[22] Helber, Steve, Associate Press, September 25, 2015. "Prominent UVA Alum Makes Controversial Donation of $50k to the McAuliffe Campaign"

[23] Faulconer, *Justin News & Advance,* January 11, 2014 "Lynchburg native Feinman a natural fit for state DNR post"

[24] At the time of writing, three quarters of the way through the year, no year 2019 grants had been published on the TROF website. They were released to the author under the Virginia Freedom of Information Act.

[25] Associated Press, May 15, 2015 "Lynchburg Native Feinman to lead Virginia tobacco commission."
https://www.newsadvance.com/news/local/lynchburg-native-feinman-to-lead-virginia-tobacco-commission/article_d0f15800-fb12-11e4-ba1f-57cee79afee4.html

expenditure and that the goal was having 40 people employed at an average annual wage of $37,000 within three years. In October Lessin signed a detailed performance agreement for a $565,000 grant committing him to return the funds to the Tobacco Commission if he failed to deliver. By June, Lessin had received at least $210,000 of the grant to develop the project.

2 FORMER BUSH FURNITURE FACTORY LOADING DOCKS IN ST PAUL

Lessin's pitch to Russell County was to use a massive, quarter million square foot facility in St Paul, Virginia to manufacture biodiesel. The modern facility in the far southwest of the state had originally been a furniture factory, and featured office space, a manufacturing floor with 24 to 30 foot high ceilings, and fiber-optic connectivity. Lessin's proposed upgrades included an active spur that could connect tanker cars with nearby Northern Southern or CSX freight rail lines. Yet in a September 2019 visit, it was obvious that the Industrial Development Authority of Russell County was still trying to get businesses into the mostly vacant facility. There was no public information available about the fate of Appalachian Biofuels LLC. What happened?

Like Ray Price before him, in 2016 Lessin privately claimed to the Tobacco Commission that a "drastic decline in world oil prices" meant that the project could not move forward. The day Lessin signed his Tobacco Commission grant application, prices were above $100 per barrel. By the time Lessin notified the commission the project was canceled, prices were under $30 per barrel.

TOBACCO COMMISSION AGAIN ABANDONS ITS FIDUCIARY RESPONSIBILITY

But that didn't mean Lessin was off the hook. Early in 2017, the Tobacco Commission notified Lessin that Appalachian Biofuels LLC now had to pay back the $565,000 grant. Lessin appealed[26] for a reduction in the "claw back" amount, but in January of 2018 was told that the Tobacco Commission Executive Committee had declined his appeal.[27] It was willing to work out a payment plan. So, on January 22, 2018 Lessin paid $355,000 of the grant back to the Tobacco Commission. That amount of the total grant was supposed to have been held in an escrow account.[28] But, with no evidence that it was, the question arises as to whether all of the grant funds were held by Lessin or Appalachian Biofuels LLC, and how repayment was made.

During the same time period, The Jerusalem Connection told the IRS it had written off $339,358 in "investment losses" after selling unspecified "assets." Although total bingo revenue was $4.2 million in 2018, net revenue had fallen from $1.2 million in 2017 to $480 thousand in 2018, with expenses exceeding revenues by $443 thousand. The Jerusalem Connection had never suffered such dire financial straits. Was a bookkeeping entry for Appalachian Biofuels LLC transferred to The

---

[26] During testimony to the Executive Committee, Charles Lessin's legal representative, Chris Nolan from the law firm McGuire Woods, testified that Lessin was at one time in possession of the entire $565,000 grant, but that "when the project was not looking good, he and the IDA agreed the best thing to do would be to put that money into escrow and I believe it's with a law firm in Southwest Virginia." The law firm was Chapin Law Firm P.C., which represents the Russell County Industrial Development Authority. The firm is led by state Senator Augustus Benton "Ben" Chapin Jr, the Russell County Republican who replaced Democrat Phillip Puckett during the prior Tobacco Commission scandal investigated by the FBI. See page 14 of the testimony referenced in the following footnote.

[27] Tobacco Region Revitalization Commission, Executive Committee Meeting, January 8, 2018, pp 10-25 https://www.revitalizeva.org/wp-content/uploads/2018/08/Executive-Committee-Meeting-Minutes-2018-01-08.pdf

[28] The author obtained records that $355,000 was paid to the Tobacco Commission in a check dated January 17, 2018 with a memo saying "All monies in Trust for Appalachian Biofuels LLL" [sic] trust account at Chapin Law Firm P.C." See http://1sraelLobby.org/Biofuels for all VFOIA documents. There is no indication how long the funds had been in the "trust" account following Lessin's transfer when "the project was not looking good."

Jerusalem Connection's balance sheet when it was already a total loss? Was the repayment of the grant really then made by The Jerusalem Connection?

The Jerusalem Connection appeared to be teetering on the edge of financial insolvency. Perhaps the Tobacco Commission grant was not held in an escrow account but rather intermingled with Lessin's other business and charitable operations. And, perhaps not wanting any negotiations for a "repayment" of the remaining $210,000 he owed the Tobacco Commission—whether from his own funds or The Jerusalem Connection—in February 2018 Lessin made an entirely new pitch. He asked the Tobacco Commission to look at the bigger picture, which Tobacco Commission Executive Director Evan Feinman memorialized in an August 5, 2019 letter:

> *In a February 2018 meeting with between (sic) TRCC staff and yourself, it was agreed that in your capacity as a member of the Virginia Israel Advisory Board, over a two-year period, you would work to meet the performance metrics promised as part of project 2941 (40 new jobs, capital investment of $3.5M) to the Commission's footprint.*

> *In July 2019, at the request of TRRC staff you provided a detailed confidential listing of the projects you have (and continue to be) involved with that are within the Commission footprint. After reviewing the locations, capital investment and jobs provided with these projects, TRRC staff can confirm that you have fully met the employment and capital investment obligations as agreed and the project can be closed. Thank you for your partnership with the Commission and please be in touch should you have any follow up questions.[29]*

Lessin likely didn't have any further questions. The bingo maven had asked Feinman to relieve him of a $210,000 obligation that should have been repaid by his small limited liability company. It was forgiven and written off solely through consideration of Lessin's position as a semi-fellow government official. Lessin's official work on a portfolio of other—some likely quite dubious— Israel-related economic development projects as a board member of VIAB, were weighed against this debt and judged to have more than covered it. Feinman then duly—without reconvening the executive committee of the Tobacco Commission, or making an announcement to the news media of the sweetheart deal, forgave Lessin's financial obligation.

---

[29] Closing Letter, Tobacco Region Revitalization Commission, August 5, 2019. See a complete copy in the Appendix.

What should have happened?

The Tobacco Commission should have sued Appalachian Biofuels LLC to repay the entire amount of the grant. Creditors of small, "closely held" LLC's like Appalachian Biofuels with one or two owners are the most likely type of LLC to have their corporate veils pierced by creditors.[30] A court can hold the owners personally liable for obligations. As the holder of a performance agreement, the Tobacco Commission could have gone after Lessin's home, bank account, investments and other assets to satisfy the terms of the agreement. A court would have certainly allowed this, since the quick collapse of global fuel prices likely would have precluded any meaningful expenditures by Lessin on biofuels production. Lessin was the perfect defendant. There was no real separation between him and the LLC. Lessin's biofuels company had recklessly failed to promptly return the grant money when it was clear the project would not proceed. The Tobacco Commission, which was supposed to invest in projects of benefit to Virginians, suffered an unjust cost under Lessin's failure to return the money.

The fact that Lessin never adequately capitalized the company and even appeared to engage in commingling assets with a charity when it was necessary to cover his losses should have led to a winning case for the Tobacco Commission. Or the U.S. Department of Justice. Or the IRS.

POP'S BINGO WORLD IN 2019

A summer 2019 visit to Pop's Bingo World reveals it has lost some of its do-gooder veneer. The surrounding area is home to check cashing storefronts, fast cash for auto title companies and hotels offering rooms for as little as $30 per night. A giant billboard steers potential customers off the main drag down Giant Drive to Pop's Bingo World.

At Pop's, the community garden to feed the needy is still advertised at the entrance, but was paved over between 2015-2016 to make way for additional parking. The latest new development is the sprawling Pop's Bar and Grill. A sports bar, the building is adjacent to the bingo hall, features 160 flat screen TVs and a "chill pit" where sports-minded customers can sprawl on overstuffed couches to view as many games as they can parse.

---

[30] NOLO, "Piercing the Corporate Veil: When LLCs and Corporations May be at Risk - An LLC or corporation's owners, members, or shareholders may be on the hook personally for business debt." https://www.nolo.com/legal-encyclopedia/personal-liability-piercing-corporate-veil-33006.html

3 POP'S BINGO WORLD BINGO HALL AND ADJOINING SPORTS BAR

The main outdoor activity these days is not gardening, but rather massive barbeque pre-game grilling fests in the outdoor lot. "We don't make any money on the food, especially the brisket," grumbles the bar tender. "The margins are all in the drinks."

One breakthrough is alcohol sales for customers in the bingo hall. If patrons order drinks at Pop's Bar and Grill, wait staff will cordially carry and pass them through a small window and into Pop's Bingo World, which, though adjacent, has no direct customer access to the new bar.

Just as in the 1980s, a September 2019 afternoon spent at Pop's is a social affair. "There's an elegant lady who shows up in her Sunday best, totally decked out," chimes the bartender. "She'll even go home after a few rounds, change, and come back in a completely different outfit. Really classy. But it can get slow at the beginning of the month. You know, people have to take care of their bills before they, you know, come down and start spending money here."

These days, even Charles Lessin is complaining publicly, telling a local news affiliate that:

> It's just not a popular game anymore...I wish I could think of other examples. Pac-Man, maybe. Pac-Man's not popular now because the other games that compete with it are so much better it's absurd. Well, that's bingo.

Lessin's Appalachian Biofuels business and its sweetheart exit deal with the Tobacco Commission never made headlines, but the Virginia Israel Advisory Board is making headlines. Seemingly every other week a new Israeli business, gathering to connect Virginia technology companies and Israeli companies in joint ventures, or yet another project at Virginia's universities in partnership with Israeli industries is announced. So, where exactly did the Virginia Israel Advisory Board come from and how does it interact with other state agencies beyond the Tobacco Region Revitalization Commission?

2.
EVOLVING JEWISH DEMOGRAPHICS IN VIRGINIA

Estimates from the 2011 DJN [Distinctive Jewish Names]
update study: Just under 10,000 Jewish persons live in 5,000
Jewish households (HH) in the Richmond, VA area. An
additional 3,100 non-Jewish persons live in these households
(24% of the total of 13,000 people in Richmond Jewish HH).
Jewish Federations of North America[31]

Overall in the United States, Jews only make up about 2.2 percent of the population.[32] The largest population concentrations are New York City, Miami, Los Angeles, Philadelphia, Chicago, San Francisco, Boston and Baltimore-Washington. As a state, Virginia is nowhere near the top of the list.

Demographics estimates about Virginia vary. The U.S. Census Bureau does not ask relevant questions about religion or ethnicity, and has not done so since the 1950s. In the race category, the 2020 census form will allow people to respond that they are white, black, or native American, as well as Chinese, Filipino, Asian Indian and other categories. Under "white" it allows respondents to elaborate, suggesting "Print, for example, German, Irish, English, Italian, Lebanese, Egyptian, etc." Theoretically, a percentage of respondents could respond "White" and then write in "Jewish" into the census response. But the result would likely be highly inconsistent, and whether or how it would be reported equally uncertain.

---

[31] The Jewish Federations of North America, "2011 DJN-based Update: Jewish Community of Richmond"
https://www.jewishdatabank.org/databank/search-results/study/583#targetText=The%202011%20Jewish%20population%20update,of%20Richmond%2Darea%20Jewish%20institutions.
[32] Pew Research Center, Religion and Public Life, A Portrait of Jewish Americans, October 1, 2013, "Population Estimates"
https://www.pewforum.org/2013/10/01/chapter-1-population-estimates/

The Jewish Virtual Library, an online resource run by former American Israel Public Affairs Committee newsletter editor Mitchell Bard, once kept close track of populations by state and claims that:

> *In 2001 approximately 66,000 residents were of the Jewish faith, comprising just 0.9 of the state's [Virginia's] total population. One of the fastest growing Jewish populations in the country, the largest Jewish community resides in Northern Virginia (35,000), followed by the Tidewater (20,000), Richmond (12,500), Roanoke (1,050), and Charlottesville (1,000). Fredericksburg, Harrisonburg, Petersburg, Staunton, and Lynchburg have small Jewish populations. Northern Virginia was once considered not a place where Jews would live, but its Jewish population has grown.[33]*

PEW'S PORTRAIT OF JEWISH AMERICANS

Pew Research stepped up to the challenge of measuring what matters to Jewish Americans when it released its "Portrait of Jewish Americans" in 2013. In it, Pew claimed, "the question of how many Jewish Americans there are does not have a simple answer. That's because the number of Jews in the U.S. depends on how one defines a Jew…" Pew settled on casting a "wide net" for the purposes of its analysis, and then allowed online users to apply filters to an interactive tool to either narrow or widen the estimated total population based on different definitions:

> *There are about **4.2 million** American adults who say they are Jewish by religion, representing 1.8% of the U.S. adult population. But there are roughly 5.3 million Jews (2.2% of the adult population) if the total also includes 'Jews of no religion,' a group of people who say they are atheist, agnostic or "nothing in particular" when asked about their religion but who were raised Jewish or have a Jewish parent and who still consider themselves Jewish aside from religion. This is the net Jewish population as defined by the Pew Research report.*

Pew's analysis of Jewish assimilation through intermarriage with non-Jews and that two-thirds of Jews claiming no religious affiliation were not raising their children as Jewish added to the alarm of Jewish

---

[33] "Jewish Virtual Library, "Virginia"
https://www.jewishvirtuallibrary.org/virginia

federation leadership, which had long been tracking the issue. Pew also claimed that 82 percent of Americans of Jewish faith did not belong to Jewish organizations. Those surveyed were only "somewhat" or "not at all" attached to Israel (70 percent) with most never having traveled there. (57 percent). Some 44 percent stated that they thought Israeli settlement building was a bad idea.

2017 GREATER WASHINGTON JEWISH COMMUNITY DEMOGRAPHIC STUDY

Perhaps alarmed by Pew's data, on February 6, 2018, one of the nation's most politically active Israel affinity organizations, the Jewish Federation of Greater Washington which covers Northern Virginia, Maryland and Washington, DC released its own survey.[34] For good reasons federations have moved away from using the term "assimilated" and "non-assimilated" as discussed in the first chapter. This Jewish federation survey report used the term "inmarried" for Jews married to Jews, and "intermarried" for households with a Jewish and a non-Jewish partner.

Some of the survey data and analysis should probably be taken with a grain of salt. The federation that sponsored it has an advocacy role and likely hopes to leverage such data into influence. Nevertheless, the results are credible, somewhat consistent with Pew and revelatory as a recent snapshot of Virginia and beyond.

The study estimates the "Greater Washington DC" Jewish community consisted of 300,000 Jewish adults and children in 2017. This population grew 37 percent between 2003 and 2017, while the overall population in the same region grew only 22 percent over the same period. This Virginia, Maryland, DC population politically identified as 72 percent Democratic Party, six percent Republican Party and 22 percent independent or other.

Their levels of education, income and professional achievement are stellar, with 92 percent having earned at least a bachelor's degree (versus only 33.4 percent of the general U.S. population) and 28 percent

---

[34] Brandeis University, Steinhardt Social Research Institute, version 1.2, March 21, 2018. "2017 Greater Washington Jewish Community Demographic Study"
https://www.brandeis.edu/ssri/pdfs/communitystudies/DCJewishCommunityStudy.pdf

holding post-graduate degrees (versus 13.1 percent of the general population).[35]

They occupy influential career positions commensurate with this advanced training, including federal, state or local government jobs (37 percent), education jobs (14 percent), science, technology, engineering and math jobs (13 percent), business and finance jobs (13 percent) the legal system, and human-service sector jobs (12 percent).

Their high rate of employment across federal, state, district or local government implies that within the survey population of Virginia, Maryland and DC 57,424 Jewish adults work inside government. If the same government participation rate holds for the entire state of Virginia, it implies 22,500 Jewish Virginians also work in government.

In terms of income, 40 percent reported an average household income of $150,000 per year, with 16 percent reporting income of greater than $250,000 yearly. In 2016 the U.S. Census Bureau reported median U.S. incomes reached their highest level ever at $59,039. Only 12 percent of the Jewish population surveyed reported their household income as less than $50,000 per year.

WEALTH, CHARITABLE GIVING AND CAMPAIGN CONTRIBUTIONS

This wealth translates into charitable giving at very high levels according to the study, with 87 percent having donated in 2017. In 2016, the overall share of American households giving to charity was estimated at around half (53.1 percent) according to a study by the University of Michigan Lilly School.[36]

If the survey asked any questions about political giving, the data and analysis were not published. However, data disclosed about household income and charitable giving can be used to make an estimate of the potential aggregate political campaign contribution power of the surveyed population.

A detailed study conducted by nonprofit software and services provider Blackbaud compared one million contributors to the 2012 election cycle from the Federal Election Commission database to its own proprietary database of 21 million U.S. households making

---

[35] U.S. Census Bureau, Educational Attainment I the United States: 2018
https://www.census.gov/data/tables/2018/demo/education-attainment/cps-detailed-tables.html

[36] 2018 Giving USA report, citing the University of Michigan Lilly School's Philanthropy Panel Study.

charitable contributions. It found 400,000 matches, and published data about the correlation between giving to charitable organizations and giving to political campaigns.[37] Blackbaud's overall conclusion was that:

> *Giving of inviduals who prize engagement—who see community action as a positive…are interested in the full political and social spectrum of how we go about achieving change."*

The study found that households with earnings at or below the median U.S. income were largely irrelevant as political campaign contributors (Accounting for 12.5 percent of total 2012 political giving.) Since 81 percent of the 155,000 Jewish households in the VA-DC-MD survey earn over $50,000, with each household 34 percent more likely to donate to charity than average households, what inferences can be drawn about this population from the perspective of Virginia state politicians?

Cross referencing the Blackbaud study with census and other data suggests that Virginia politicians targeting "campaign contribution relevant" households within nearly three million state households would encounter approximately 860,000 households of interest. The vast majority of them (800,000) would be non-Jewish and 60,000 would identify as Jewish. The total potential annual campaign contributions of relevant Virginia households, cross referencing Census and Blackbaud data would be $115 million per year. The correlation between higher charitable giving and greater household wealth would make Jewish household campaign contribution potential in Virginia nearly $25 million per year, vs $90 million for all other campaign contribution relevant households.

This means that just seven percent of campaign contribution relevant households could deliver 28 percent of total potential contributions. A great number of these households would likely prefer giving to Democratic Party candidates. But what specific issues would politicians perceive they needed to emphasize in order to tap that segment?

According to the Jewish Federation of Greater Washington survey of Virginia, Maryland and DC, the affinity for Israel of the state of Virginia may be higher than the national average explored by Pew

---

[37] Blackbaud, May 23, 2016, "Giving in an Election Year"
https://merkleresponse.com/sites/default/files/blog/giving-in-an-election-year.pdf

Research in 2013. Some 68 percent of the region's Jewish residents have been to Israel at least once, and 4 percent of the population surveyed actually have Israeli citizenship. Over half—54 percent of the population—claim close family or friends live in Israel.

Given these more geographically focused data points, it is reasonable to assume the professional, wealthy, highly educated Jewish population of the Virginia, Maryland, DC area is by nature one of the most heavily courted and listened to by politicians—and that politicians emphasize "support for Israel" as their default setting. A Virginia politician probably believes that taking a proactive position on the Israel issue might provide entry into a potential $25 million annual Virginia campaign contribution bucket, perhaps intuitively without knowing particular numbers.

The Jewish Federation of Greater Washington survey validates one of Pew's 2013 conclusions, "...due to lack of interest or lack of opportunity, nearly half of Jewish households and families remain largely disconnected from the organized Jewish community."[38] But that does not make it an un-addressable community that lacks interconnectivity and internal communication channels. That is because, according to the survey:

> *Personal friendships and interactions are important to the Jews of Greater Washington. The vast majority (95%) of Jews in Metro DC have at least some friends who are Jewish, and 60% say at least half of their closest friends are Jewish. Informal and cultural activities include Jewish activities and participation in Jewish life outside of the framework of organizations. Discussing Jewish topics was the most common activity, followed by eating Jewish foods and seeking information about Judaism online. Jewish culture includes reading Jewish books, listening to Jewish music, or attending Jewish performances or museums.[39]*

---

[38] Brandeis University, Steinhardt Social Research Institute, version 1.2, March 21, 2018. p. 83 "2017 Greater Washington Jewish Community Demographic Study"
https://www.brandeis.edu/ssri/pdfs/communitystudies/DCJewishCommunityStudy.pdf

[39] Brandeis University, Steinhardt Social Research Institute, version 1.2, March 21, 2018. p. 65 "2017 Greater Washington Jewish Community Demographic Study"

Israel advocacy to generate Jewish community support in the form of campaign contributions is likely a "no-brainer" for Virginia politicians. But what about the growing numbers within the Democratic Party base—including Jews—that hold increasingly negative views about Israel because of its policies?

In an April 1-15 2019 Pew Research Center poll, 61 percent of Republicans held favorable views of the Israeli government while 67 percent of Democrats held unfavorable views.[40] The issue seems like a clear example of a bona fide difference between two parties that have somewhat indistinguishable policies when it comes to endless war, interventionist foreign policy, and deference to big business and Wall Street.

AN ADDRESSABLE "ISRAEL ACCOUNTABILITY" DEMOGRAPHIC?

Could grassroots Democrats in Virginia and elsewhere be courted through "hold Israel accountable" messaging from politicians seeking to pressure that country on its human rights issues and motivate a fair deal with Palestinians? On the surface, the overall environment seems increasingly favorable. In general, the majority in the country believe U.S. aid to Israel is excessive, with 58 percent saying it was "too much" in 2018, and 60.2 percent saying the same thing in 2019.[41] So why don't any Virginia Democratic Party politicians aspiring for state office target this potentially large voting population via "hold Israel accountable" messaging?

One reason may be that politicians probably believe that any move in that direction would mean permanently dashing hopes of receiving support from Virginia's establishment Jewish campaign contributor segment that holds high affinity for Israel. And the challenges in finding and addressing potential Jewish dissidents and non-Jewish donors within the $90 million general campaign contributor segment are daunting.

---

https://www.brandeis.edu/ssri/pdfs/communitystudies/DCJewishCommun ityStudy.pdf

[40] Pew Research Center, April 24, 2109 "U.S. Public Has Favorable View of Israel's People, but Is Less Positive Toward Its Government," https://www.people-press.org/2019/04/24/u-s-public-has-favorable-view-of-israels-people-but-is-less-positive-toward-its-government/

[41] IRmep polls on American adult support for U.S. aid to Israel conducted through Google Surveys, 2017-2018, https://IRmep.org/polls/

If 60 percent are generally in favor of cutting aid to Israel, they represent an addressable donor market of $54 million. This is consistent with polling that suggests that up to 30 percent of Virginia's population are evangelical Protestants holding strong beliefs that supporting Israel is a religious mandate. [42]

But if the hypothetical politician wanted to launch campaign messaging to the remaining members of the pool, he or she would probably have to position excessive foreign aid and unconditional support to Israel within an acceptable category in order to communicate with voters and pass muster with mass media outlets. If the politician framed aid to Israel as a "government/poor leadership" issue, polling data suggests that would resonate as the top issue for only 24 percent of the population.[43] But even if completely successful, it reduces the hypothetical **addressable campaign contribution pool to only $13 million.** The politician would also quickly discover there is not really any efficient way to tap existing networks to communicate with this segment. Aside from a few loosely organized human rights groups with email lists and Facebook pages, there are not many means for efficiently communicating with people wanting to support politicians determined to hold Israel more accountable.

Another challenge facing any politician attempting to legislate policies for the "accountability" segment is that such policies would likely be defeated before they were fully drafted. With 22,500 Jewish Virginians working in various levels of government and 76 percent holding emotional attachments to Israel (17,100), given the high levels of intercommunication, word about accountability measures would spread quickly, and effective countermeasures might become the topic of the week.

Word would also likely quickly get back to stakeholders in Israel. Some of these messages might even be sent by Israelis. That is because if 4 percent of the Virginia state (like the greater VA-MD-DC) Jewish population are also Israeli citizens, with a connection beyond emotional attachment to Israel, word would also quickly spread to that country by the estimated 684 concerned Israeli dual citizens holding Virginia government jobs. This all might be why the "default" setting for

---

[42] Pew Research Center, Religion and Public Life, Adults in Virginia, "Religious composition of adults in Virginia," https://www.pewforum.org/religious-landscape-study/state/virginia/

[43] Gallup poll, March-September 2019 average percentage of Americans, "Most Important Problem" https://news.gallup.com/poll/1675/most-important-problem.aspx

Virginia politicians is mostly automatic, robust support for Israel. Of course, robust automatic support for Israel alone is insufficient to win Jewish voters. That has already been convincingly demonstrated.

President Donald Trump officially recognized Jerusalem as Israel's capital, installed a slate of hardliner Israel partisans to negotiate an Israel Palestine settlement, and recognized Israel's sovereignty over Syria's Golan Heights. None of this caused any significant defection of Jewish Democratic Party supporters who vote with Democrats because they are not single issue voters and also care deeply about health care, social justice, immigrant welfare and climate change.[44]

UNLIMITED CORPORATE AND INDIVIDUAL CAMPAIGN CONTRIBUTIONS

Also, the Virginia campaign contribution scene and political calculations are much more complicated than the extrapolations presented above. Within the 24 percent of greater Washington Jews not holding any emotional attachment to Israel, some are very "detached" indeed and actively working with likeminded fellow Jews and others to hold Israel accountable. These individuals and their extended community can easily be contacted at groups such as Jewish Voice for Peace.

Also, not only are Virginia politicians tapping contributors from across the United States, Virginia is among a handful of states that allow direct, unlimited campaign contributions by anyone under state election law. That means all individuals and corporations whether located in Virginia or not.

Candidate for governor Terry McAuliffe received two out of state donations totaling more than a million dollars that looked like down-payments on pro-Israel policy. The first was $572,636 from Haim Saban, producer of the "Power Rangers" franchise whose most famous quote is, "I'm a one-issue guy, and my issue is Israel." In 2003, after Saban donated $7 million to the Democratic National Committee,

---

[44] NPR, Morning Edition, August 22, 2019, "Trump's 'Disloyalty' Claim About Jewish Democrats Shows He Doesn't Get How They Vote" https://www.npr.org/2019/08/22/753131249/trumps-disloyalty-claim-about-jewish-democrats-shows-he-doesn-t-get-how-they-vot

then-party chairman McAuliffe called Saban and told him, "you're the man!"[45]

The other gubernatorial race donor was $776,076 from billionaire JB Pritzker who is now the elected governor of Illinois and longtime supporter of pro-Israel charities such as Friends of the IDF, which builds recreational facilities for Israel's military.

Across the United States, compiling lists of vocal, billionaire pro-Israel Jewish political mega contributors are easy and has become a bit of a cliché. Sheldon Adelson, Michael Bloomberg, Paul Singer, Bernard Marcus, Seth Klarman, Daniel Abraham, Leslie Wexner, Irving Moskowitz, Stephen Spielberg.[46]

In contrast, if there are as many Jewish mega-donors using their wealth to influence politicians to hold Israel accountable, they are not yet widely publicly known. If they do exist, they probably contribute privately to non-profits or dark money groups rather than as individuals or corporations in a manner that is publicly disclosed. To do otherwise would be to place oneself at risk of being ostracized, boycotted, labeled anti-Semitic or a self-hating Jew, or marginalized in other ways.

Although foreign nationals are technically banned by federal law from contributing to political campaigns, there is little standing in the way of a U.S.-incorporated subsidiary of a foreign corporation making a significant contribution to Virginia politicians.[47] Many Virginia state legislators are in "constant campaign mode," some receive tens of thousands of dollars per week from corporations and individuals. Spending by "dark money" groups that claim not to coordinate with candidates, but which invest additional millions in advertising including social media campaigns, further complicate any watchdog efforts to link campaign contributions to legislation and other political action made on behalf of the contributor.

---

[45] Daunt, Tina, Los Angeles Times, April 22, 2009, "Loyal friend to Israel and Democrats" https://www.latimes.com/archives/la-xpm-2009-apr-22-et-cause22-story.html

[46] OpenSecrets.org, Top Individual Contributors, All Federal Elections, https://www.opensecrets.org/overview/topindivs.php

[47] Schwarz, Jon, The Intercept, June 1, 2016, "VA Gov. Terry McAuliffe Took $120k From A Chinese Billionaire — But The Crime Is That It Was Legal" https://theintercept.com/2016/06/01/va-gov-terry-mcauliffe-took-120k-from-a-chinese-billionaire-but-the-crime-is-that-it-was-legal/

3.
WHERE DID VIAB COME FROM? JEWISH FEDERATIONS AND CITIZEN LOBBYISTS

There's no state that has an agency that is funded by the state. There's [sic] probably 20 states that have some type of Israel-America Chamber of Commerce. ... but it's nothing that's funded by the state. It's got a little bit of gravitas. But it doesn't have the gravitas if the state doesn't do anything about it. **Dov Hoch, Executive Director of the Virginia Israel Advisory Board**[48]

The organized Jewish community in Virginia began to forge ties between the state government and Israel in earnest in the mid-1980s. This was a period of immense economic difficulty within Israel's economy. At the national level, the American Israel Public Affairs Committee worked to unilaterally lower all tariffs against Israeli products entering the United States, thinking exports could provide a boost to the ailing Israeli agricultural and manufacturing industries. It pushed what was billed as the first modern "free trade agreement" through Congress. The FTA kept U.S. companies locked out of Israel's market while unilaterally dropping U.S. tariffs.

In Virginia, the "Virginia Israel Commission" emerged in 1986 to promote deeper bilateral economic ties to Israel. In 1988 Governor Gerald Baliles signed a formal agreement with Israel, but the commission's activities dwindled until 1995. That year Governor George Allen created the new Virginia-Israel Partnership to focus additional resources on promoting trade as well as art, education and general government."[49] But yet another executive agreement didn't have adequate legal underpinnings to institutionalize a permanent body dedicated to improving Israel's

---

[48] Hoch, Dov, "What VIAB Does and How it Benefits Virginia," speech at the Weinstein Jewish Community Center, Richmond, VA, April 4, 2019. Introduction and remarks by former president of the Jewish Federation of Richmond Nathan Shor

[49] Jewish Virtual Library, State-to-State Cooperation: Virginia and Israel https://www.jewishvirtuallibrary.org/virginia-israel-cooperation

economy from within Virginia state government. Virginia-Israel ties were subject to shifting political winds and drift. That all stopped with the arrival on the scene by Eric Cantor.

Eric Cantor's most widely known achievements came from his time in the U.S. congress as a stalwart promoter of Israel and his almost becoming the first Jewish Speaker of the House. As Cantor worked his way into the position of House Majority Leader, he labored mightily to cut off all U.S. foreign assistance to Palestinians. In meetings with Israeli Prime Minister Benjamin Netanyahu, Cantor pledged that Republicans would "serve as a check" on any Obama administration pressure on Israel. Cantor was ultimately ousted in 2014 in a surprising upset by tea party candidate David Brat.

Before he took to the national stage, Cantor served in the Virginia House of Delegates between 1992 to 2001 representing the 73rd district, a corner northwest of Richmond. In 1996, Cantor helped pass legislation creating a permanent new executive agency within the Virginia's Governor's office, the Virginia-Israel Advisory Board, as chronicled by *Washington Jewish Week*:

> *The father of the advisory board was then-delegate and later House Majority Leader Eric Cantor (R-Va.), who proposed the body in 1996. The board consists of 31 members, most of whom are volunteers.*[50]

Arguably, VIAB's creation may have been a more permanent accomplishment for Israel than any of Cantor's later achievements in the U.S. House of Representatives. But what exactly is VIAB?

VIAB'S ORIGINAL ADVISORY BOARD CHARTER

VIAB's original charter shared common themes of its predecessor organizations. It was to "advise the Governor on ways to improve economic and cultural links between the Commonwealth and the State of Israel, with a focus on the areas of commerce and trade, art and education, and general government."

Unlike its predecessors, VIAB had permanence and functioned within the office of the governor between 1996 and 2018 and had a salaried executive director, a small state-funded annual budget and additional support from the governor's staff.

---

[50] Katz, Justin, *Washington Jewish Week*, May 25, 2017, "Va. business rep doing his last Israel deals" https://washingtonjewishweek.com/38867/va-biz-rep-doing-his-last-israel-deals/featured-right/

VIAB's board members were volunteers appointed by either the governor, state senate or the state house. Under law, four of the 29-citizen members were required to be drawn from four Virginia-based Jewish community federations. Jewish federations are fundraising and citizen lobbying operations present in every major U.S. population center. In 2012 federations raised $947 million, had nearly 8,000 employees and nearly 60,000 volunteers.[51] They functioned within a larger $3.4 billion Israel affinity ecosystem of organizations subsidizing Israel ($2 billion), conducting pro-Israel advocacy ($400 million), and engaging in education as defined by federations ($317 million). [52]

Federations and their internal, usually integrated Jewish Community Relations Councils exert coordinated pressure on the local news media, influencers, and members of state legislatures. Little of it is visible, and key to their success is lack of public awareness. Douglas Bloomfield is a former AIPAC lobbyist once investigated by the FBI for his role while working at AIPAC in the 1984 theft of American corporate trade secrets in league with an Israeli diplomat that helped produce America's worst bilateral trade deal.[53] Bloomfield sounded an alarm over the potentially negative impact of an Obama administration proposal that would have called for public disclosure of the actual amount of meetings—as opposed to reported expenditures on—federation JCRC citizen lobbying, writing that:

> *The president's proposal to 'require lobbyists to disclose each contact' may result in treating 'citizen lobbying' by groups such as local Jewish community relations councils the same as corporate and labor interests. The proposals in Obama's State of the Union address to 'require lobbyists to disclose each contact' with Congress or the administration on behalf of a client will create an avalanche of paperwork for the small groups that can least afford it. On the surface the president did not call for restricting the activities of unpaid volunteers who engage in grassroots lobbying for nonprofit groups, which is critical for most Jewish charitable organizations. But that could be the result if he succeeds in removing the current exemption from*

---

[51] Smith, Grant F. 2016, IRmep, Washington, D.C. pages 308-312, "Big Israel, How Israel's Lobby Moves America"

[52] Smith, Grant F. 2016, IRmep, Washington, D.C. page 317, "Big Israel, How Israel's Lobby Moves America."

[53] IRmep.org, Israel Lobby Archive, "FBI investigates AIPAC for espionage and theft of government property in 1984.
http://www.IsraelLobby.org/economy

> *registration for groups where less than one-fifth of the lobbyist's
> time is spent lobbying.*
>
> *Disclosure: I am biased. I've spent many years lobbying, mostly
> for Jewish organizations and causes. They depend on a
> grassroots network of deeply committed, well-informed citizen
> lobbyists; many are also campaign contributors, which already
> requires detailed reporting to the Federal Election Commission.
> In this era of gotcha politics and 24/7 cable media, it's easy to
> imagine a report of lobbyist contacts being used by an
> incumbent's opponents to attack him or her as a tool of the
> special interests. Some lawmakers may be hounded into also
> producing lists of unpaid / unregistered lobbyists, including
> constituents, they meet, even though there are no plans to require
> such disclosure, according to a source close to the White House.
> That could easily inhibit the willingness of lawmakers to meet
> ...with constituents and discourage participation by citizen
> lobbyists who fear becoming public targets.*

The four Jewish federations statutorily empowered to provide
unpaid volunteers to VIAB's board are the Jewish Community
Federation of Richmond,[54] the Jewish Community Relations Council
of Greater Washington, United Jewish Federation of Tidewater, and
the United Jewish Community of the Virginia Peninsula. They raise
approximately $33.6 million per year. In comparison, United Way
campaigns in Virginia, according to the sum of their most recently
available filings, raise about $100 million annually in the state, with the
Richmond United Way alone contributing $19 million.

---

[54] The Jewish Community Relations Committee (JCRC) of the Jewish
Community Federation of Richmond (JCFR) states that it is "the central
public affairs arm of the organized Jewish community and focuses its
programs and advocacy on four pillars;
1. Promoting religious freedom and the separation of church and
   state,
2. Supporting a democratic, strong and peaceful Israel, as the
   homeland and nation-state of the Jewish people,
3. The eradication of all forms of racism and anti-Semitism,
4. The safety and well-being of Jewish agencies, organizations, and
   individuals in the Richmond community and environs."

Federation	Revenues (million)	Employees	Volunteers
Jewish Community Federation of Richmond (Figures include the co-located Richmond Jewish Foundation)	$7.2	19	158
Jewish Community Relations Council and Federation of Greater Washington.[55]	$15.2	35	2,860
United Jewish Federation of Tidewater (Virginia Beach)	$7.3	5	0
United Jewish Community of The Virginia Peninsula (Newport News, figures include endowment.)	$3.9	74	55
Total	$33.6	133	3,073

4 VIRGINIA JEWISH FEDERATION FUNDRAISING, EMPLOYEES AND VOLUNTEERS

Like other such Jewish federations operating across the nation, Virginia's are very heavily politically involved in advocating for Israel. They raise funds for direct transfers to "friends of Israel" charities that send funds on to Israeli universities, nonprofits, and other such entities. On the politics front, they host candidate forums which pit competitors from the same party to "out-support Israel" each other.

Like other Jewish federations, these charities uniformly claim to the IRS on annual tax returns that they do not engage in any "direct or indirect political campaign activities" or any lobbying activities. But the federations providing board members to VIAB are extremely politically active, as well as their donors and administrators. They are the reason VIAB exists.

The official mission of a Jewish federation is to enhance Jewish communal life. The mission of the Jewish Community Federation of Richmond, for example, is to:

---

[55] Since this region includes portions of Maryland and Washington, DC as well as northern Virginia, revenue, employees and staff member figures presented here are divided by one-third.

interest itself in all matters pertaining to the Jewish community in the city of Richmond and its vicinity and in and outside of the Commonwealth of Virginia, and to be helpful in such ways as are to the best interest of all persons of the Jewish faith.[56]

But their quiet activities have state-wide ramifications. Early in 2018, the Virginia federations attempted to ram through a series of controversial changes to Virginia K-12 textbooks with the help of a California based Israel advocacy organization called the "Institute for Curriculum Services." Their proposed edits to McGraw Hill, Prentice Hall, National Geographic and other publisher textbooks demanded they teach students that Israel does not occupy any foreign territory and that Arabs alone have been responsible for all crisis initiation in Middle East conflicts, among other false claims. The federation letters accompanying packets of proposed changes leveraged their presumed influence, affirming that, "we know ICS looks forward to working with all of the publishers to make appropriate edits to the texts."[57]

The federations were quiet about their initiative, submitting change requests[58] by cover letter to the Virginia Department of Education and pages of supporting documentation right before a deadline for community input on the state textbook adoption process.[59]

---

[56] Jewish Community Federation of Richmond, 2017 IRS Form 990, filed on November 11, 2018.

[57] See the Appendix.

[58] IRmep.org, Israel Lobby Archive, February 28, 2018 "The Institute for Curriculum Services (ICS) formally requests changes to Virginia textbooks and teacher guides in coordination with Jewish Community Relations Councils (JCRCs)"https://IsraelLobby.org/ICS/

[59] Jewish Community Federation of Richmond, Letter to Christonya Brown, History and Social Science Coordinator, Office of Humanities and Early Childhood , Virginia Department of Education, February, 28, 2018 https://IsraelLobby.org/ics/Letter_to_VA_DOE_from_Jewish_Communiti es_of_VA_on_2018_Textbook_Adoption.pdf

> Volume 2, Topic 12: New Nations Emerge (1945-present), Lesson 4: Conflict in the Middle East, Israel and Palestine, The Difficult Road to Peace, page 608, right column, paragraph 1, lines 6-8, **Change:** "Arabs referred to these lands as the "occupied territories." Later, Israel annexed East Jerusalem and the Golan Heights. Israel then allowed Jewish settlers to build homes the building of homes and communities in some of these territories areas, which the Palestinians opposed."
> **Comments:** Good pedagogy requires that material is presented neutrally, accurately, and in context. The terms "occupied territories" and "settlers" are loaded terms and politicized words, favoring a particular perspective. Jews have had a continuous presence in the region. There were Jewish communities in these areas until 1948, when the Jewish residents fled or were expelled by Arab fighters. Additionally, as noted in the accompanying interactive map analysis, Sinai, Gaza, and parts of the West Bank later returned to Egyptian and Palestinian control. Use of the term "bitterness," an expression of emotion, exclusively for the Palestinian point of view lacks balance. The conflict is a highly emotional issue for Israelis and Palestinians. The recommended change offers a more neutral description.

5 VIRGINIA JEWISH FEDERATION AND ICS PROPOSED CHANGES TO THE PEARSON WORLD HISTORY AND GEOGRAPHY TEXTBOOK

VIRGINIA'S OTHER ADVISORY BOARDS

Virginia is home to other advisory boards, but none come even close to the power and influence of VIAB. The Virginia Latino Advisory Board was formed in 2005 to advise the governor on "economic, professional, cultural, educational, and governmental links between the Commonwealth of Virginia, the Latino community in Virginia, and Latin America." While VIAB directly mandates one leader or designee from four establishment Jewish federations have a position on VIAB's board, VLAB is even more direct. Fifteen of its twenty-one non-legislative citizen members, according to its enabling state law, "shall be of Latino descent."

VLAB's programs are those of an economically and politically challenged population making up nine percent of Virginians. It works on legislation to increase affordable housing, decrease evictions, and create more diversity in state government employment. They are not political players in the campaign contribution arena. The total campaign contributions of VLAB board members 2017-2018 amount to less than $10,000.

The Virginia Asian Advisory Board, formed in 2001, has a similar mission, representing close to 600,000 Virginians of Asian descent. Its mission includes forging economic ties with Pacific Rim nations, a vastly less focused endeavor than VIAB's mission. The group hosted a 2017 summit at George Mason University called "Advocating for the Interests of Asians Across the Commonwealth." The group urged increased trade with Asian countries, greater civic engagement but also basic needs such as help overcoming barriers to education and English proficiency. VAAB board members made $32,000 in 2017-2018 campaign contributions. Eleven of VAAB's 21 members must "be of Asian descent" according to the law that created it.

The most recent entry into Virginia's community advisory boards was the formation of the Virginia African American Advisory Board in 2019. In an understatement, Delegate Lamont Bagby said, "The creation of this board is far overdue." Representing 20 percent of the state's population, fifteen members of the 21 legislatively appointed citizen members of the board, "must be African American." Between the years 2020 and 2025, the Virginia Department of Planning and Budget estimates the office won't have expenditures greater than $8,400 annually.[60]

This community has no museum to educate fellow Virginians about the state's role in the enslavement and exploitation of African Americans. Lawrence Douglas Wilder is a lawyer who became the first elected African American governor of a U.S. state since Reconstruction, serving Virginia from 1990 to 1994. In 2009 he founded the United States National Slavery Museum in Fredericksburg, Virginia. Founded based on a vision he unveiled in 2001, the museum was to house a full-scale slave ship replica, a theater and library with an expected two million people visiting each year.

But it never fully came to fruition. A garden created in 2007 now lies "covered in thick snarls of thorns and vines" and is "strangled by weeds and debt."[61] While just 74 miles to the north, the National Museum of African American History and Culture did finally open its doors in 2016, Virginia's approach to the subject is scattershot, with collections mainly hosted within larger entities, such as the Black History Museum and Cultural Center of Virginia and Virginia Museum of History and Culture. This lack of prioritization and ongoing battles to honestly depict the impact of slavery in state textbooks reflect the continued marginalization of the Black community in Virginia.

From the perspective of makeup, timing of their launch and programs, the creation of these "fellow" advisory boards differ greatly from VIAB while giving VIAB cover for one of its most interesting

---

[60] Virginia's Legislative Information System, Department of Planning and Budget 2019 Fiscal Impact Statement, HB2767, Virginia African American Advisory Board https://lis.virginia.gov/cgi-bin/legp604.exe?191+oth+HB2767F122+PDF

[61] Atlas Obscura, "Abandoned National Slavery Museum: An overgrown garden stands as a grim marker of an unrealized dream." https://www.atlasobscura.com/places/abandoned-united-states-national-slavery-museum

aspects—a presence of Jewish establishment leadership via state mandated quota and majority board membership by Jewish activists.

The Jewish federations that created VIAB have been around a long time. Richmond's dates back to 1942, Virginia Peninsula 1971 and Greater Washington 1953. It would have been problematic and counterproductive for its enabling legislation to state that "most of VIAB's members must be upstanding Jewish citizen activists dedicated to advancing Israel." Since the goal of forming VIAB was generating political influence inside government to economically aid Israel and VIAB board members, the quota mandates a Jewish federation role through four designated members. That alone does not, like the later boards created by state law, ensure that the majority of members serving on VIAB's board are Jewish. And yet they are.

The Jewish Federations of North America, umbrella of all American Jewish federations, uses a specific procedure to identify the numbers of Jews within any given population called "distinctive Jewish names," or DJN. The Jewish Federations of North America obtains and electronic listing of names and then compares them to a database of DJNs.[62] For example, when the JFN performed this lookup in 2011, its stated key findings were:

> *Estimates from the 2011 DJN update study: Just under 10,000 Jewish persons live in 5,000 Jewish households (HH) in the Richmond, VA area. An additional 3,100 non-Jewish persons live in these households (24% of the total of 13,000 people in Richmond Jewish HH).*

Applying the DJN process[63] to a list of VIAB board members serving between 2005-2018 reveals that 68 percent are Jewish. However, since many Jewish board members serve multiple terms and non-Jews serve fewer multiple terms, Jews are occupying appointed VIAB board seats 80 percent of the time.

---

[62] The Jewish Federations of North America, "2011 DJN-based Update: Jewish Community of Richmond"
https://www.jewishdatabank.org/databank/search-results/study/583#targetText=The%202011%20Jewish%20population%20update,of%20Richmond%2Darea%20Jewish%20institutions.

[63] It is the author's view that the DJN methodology is imprecise even when used to estimate large populations. Wherever possible the application of DJN to the VIAB board members on the list was supplemented by reviewing member biographies and public statements to boost accuracy.

Virginia Board	Background	Percentage	Means
Virginia Asian Advisory Board	Asian American	86%	Quota
Virginia Latino Advisory Board	Latino American	71%	Quota
Virginia African American Advisory Board	African American	71%	Quota
Virginia Israel Advisory Board	Jewish American	80%	Other

6 ETHNO-RELIGIOUS VIRGINIA STATE BOARD MEMBER PARTICIPATION BY QUOTA OR OTHER

This means that while the other board quotas require an average ethnic participation rate by law averaging 76 percent, VIAB's Jewish participation rate is four percent higher. Since Jewish participation quotas are not statutorily mandated in VIAB's enabling law, what is causing this greater ethno-religious concentration, and does it have any downsides?

One can reasonably assume a great deal of state legislative appointments are motivated by VIAB member campaign contributions. Marcus Weinstein, in addition to his impressive philanthropic accomplishments, can probably rest easy that his nearly $300,000 in campaign contributions buys him enough sway with his state representative to guarantee multiple terms. The same umbrella likely creates opportunities for Jewish members who don't make many contributions. If Marcus, Gottschalk or Lessin recommend fellow Jews to be nominated, it likely carries a great deal of weight.

While non-Jews obviously also serve as members on the board, they do not appear to offer any adversarial views or criticism, at least, not as revealed in official board minutes. Non-Jewish members can apparently become dissidents. Todd Patterson Haymore was a designated member of VIAB's board serving three terms (2010-2011, 2011-2012 and 2016-2017). But his views that VIAB's self-proclaimed contributions to Virginia's tax revenue were "inflated without merit" only came as he was exiting state government, and only to a small circle of non-VIAB state government employees. It has had no impact on VIAB continuing to claim large benefits to Virginia without providing any substantiations of its widely touted numbers. It also seems unlikely that any legislator or governor would appoint a non-VIAB vetted, knowledgeable public watchdog adversary to the VIAB board for the reasons explored in the discussion about Virginia's campaign contributions realities in Chapter 2.

So, one important downside to VIAB's board membership homogeneity is an overwhelming culture of non-self-criticism and aversion to adversarial views. This VIAB has the power to impact Virginia's economy in similar ways to the legislature or Virginia Economic Development Partnership, and yet it has none of their built-in checks and balances.

In contrast, Virginia's Asian American community and its board is anything but homogeneous despite the quota, hailing from different cultures, countries, religions and languages from across a vast region. VAAB did not form as an agency of a unified power bloc in Virginia, and therefore its state mandated quota is based on ethnicity, and not association with any state based interest group. The same can be said for the Virginia Latino Advisory Board.

What the Asian and Latino boards do provide is cover for VIAB. They allow board members to say, "see, this is a normal thing in Virginia. Other ethno religious groups are forming boards too." This is, of course, not true. The Asian and Latino boards did not come out of programs and policy objectives of large, established, empowered interest groups. Their objectives are those of fragmented communities struggling for basic needs, without the wealth and networks of well-formed interest groups. They are also still struggling to define their own identity, with the Asian board working to further sub-segment its membership to better understand its own diversity. These state boards aren't forming out of grassroots empowerment.

In February of 2019, Governor Ralph Northam faced widespread calls for resignation, including from the Virginia Legislative Caucus after photos emerged from a 1984 medical school yearbook. One photo on his yearbook page portrayed a student in Ku Klux Klan robes, alongside another student in blackface. After initially taking responsibility for the photo, he later denied that it was him, though he admitted applying the same type of makeup to portray Michael Jackson in a dance contest.

Northam made efforts to repair relations by attending a symposium on the role of historically black colleges and universities as a note-taking participant. He also hired a "Director of Diversity, Equity and Inclusion" to address unequal treatment in state government. Taken together, supporting the creation of and appointing a governor's board, conducting understanding tours, and hiring for diversity awareness can be seen as top-down attempts to repair his image when it comes to state race relations.

In 2014 Democratic Party senator Chap Petersen representing Fairfax and environs (whose wife was of Korean descent) and Korean American Lawyer Mark Keam (D-Vienna) filed draft legislation to create the "Virginia-Korea Advisory Board" modeled on VIAB.[64] Hoping to leverage the presence of "100,000 Korean Americans living in Virginia" as a base, the pair wanted to obtain a budget and springboard the new entity into existence. The effort failed. None of the preconditions that allowed VIAB to come into being exist in this community. Although there is a significant population base in Falls Church and Annandale, there is little visible community organizing or culture of nonprofit giving. The nonprofit Korean American Society of Virginia focuses on education, but raises less than $100,000 per year. The Korean-American Association of Greater Washington does not even appear to be incorporated or raising funds.

VIAB BOARD MEMBER CAUSES AND CAMPAIGN CONTRIBUTIONS

Campaign contributions are central to VIAB's political power and influence. Overall, VIAB board members have contributed more than $1.5 million to state politicians from 2005-2018 according to data available on the Virginia Public Access Project campaign contribution database.[65]

Virginia real estate mogul and VIAB board member Marcus M. Weinstein has career campaign contributions to state politicians totaling nearly $300,000. Weinstein has been appointed to the VIAB board by the state house from 2008-2018. He started out in 1952 building single-family homes around Richmond and expanded into apartment buildings and commercial real estate. His Weinstein Properties manages more than 18,000 apartments.

Along with his wife, Carole, Marcus Weinstein gives heavily (25.5 million) to the University of Richmond, their alma mater. He chairs the Virginia Holocaust Museum and gives heavily to the Richmond federation and its Jewish Community Relations Council building bears his name. They also gave $5 million to build a cyber security engineering building which also bears their name at Ben-Gurion

---

[64] Delegate Mark Keam, Virginia's 35th House District, media release, January 14, 2014, "Announcing Bills to Create Virginia-Korea Advisory Board to Bring Jobs and Develop Economic Partnership" https://markkeam.com/?q=node/52583

[65] Virginia Public Access Project, https://vpap.org

University in Israel.[66] Weinstein gave heavily to elect Governor Ralph Northam ($35,000) and like many other VIAB board members prioritized giving to fellow VIAB board member Eileen Filler-Corn's election campaign for the House of Delegates ($12,500).

The Virginia General Assembly provided the current building—the American Tobacco Company Warehouse—for the Virginia Holocaust Museum in Richmond. It is located on prime riverfront property and undergoing renovations expected to be completed in 2020.

Eileen Filler-Corn ran for Democratic Party delegate in 2010 and since served in the crucial 41st district of Fairfax County. If VIAB board members have anything in common, it was their support for her run. In addition to Weinstein, she received campaign contributions from Richard S. Samet ($4,630), Mel Chaskin, ($1,000), Charles Lessin ($500) and Steven David Stone ($3,074) for a total of $46,282 in fellow VIAB board member contributions. Emphasizing support for public schools in her run, Filler-Corn could be key to the success of winning contracts for Energix in Northern Virginia.

Long-time military contractor Mel Chaskin became a member of the VIAB board through sequential two-year appointments by the state house since the year 2005. Becoming chairman then requires only a routine, perfunctory nomination, seconded and the passed by VIAB board members voting at a meeting. Chaskin as always received those nominations and votes, and only ever served as Chairman. He has given nearly $80,000 to politicians across the state, from small mayoral races to county boards of supervisors. There is an almost transitional relationship in the gradual winding down of Chaskin's U.S. military contracting and the rise of Oran Safety Glass, as explored later. What is unknowable to any but Vanguard Research insiders are whether the company has been secretly doing paid work with Israeli military contractors to transfer operations to Virginia that are then implemented by VIAB. Chaskin's leadership of VIAB is a clear indication of its dedication to not just Israeli companies, but Israeli military contractors.

VIAB, like most of the Jewish federations, has close ties the American Israel Public Affairs Committee. Irving M. Blank, who lists his work for VIAB as "1996-present" was a member of AIPAC's national council as well as the National Jewish Community Relations Council. He is a personal injury attorney at Blank and Marcus. A

---

[66] American Associates of Ben-Gurion University, November 20, 2014, "Carole and Marcus Weinstein Building Named at BGU" https://aabgu.org/carole-marcus-weinstein-building-named-bgu/#

departing, young, disgruntled staff member of AIPAC—after proving
his own bona fides—a few years ago told the author that federations
and JCRCs serve as "lily pads" for astroturfing AIPAC initiatives across
the country.

Board member Sam Asher is the Executive Director of Richmond's
Holocaust Museum. Before signing on, he raised $23 million for the
Jewish Federation of Delaware and is Executive Director of the Jewish
Community Federation.

Former Republican Party Governor of Virginia George Allen has
also served as a VIAB board member (2005-2008). In 2006 while
finishing his first term in the U.S. Senate, he ran for a second term
against Democratic Party nominee Jim Webb, former Secretary of the
Navy and retired Air Force officer Gail Parker. Allen torpedoed his
own campaign on August 11, 2006 during a campaign stop on the
Kentucky border. He accused a man taking video of his event, S. R.
Sidarth, of being a "tracker" for opponent Webb. He used the term
"macaca" meaning "monkey" referring to the dark complexioned
Sidarth and implying he was not a Virginia native:

> *This fellow here over here with the yellow shirt, Macaca, or
> whatever his name is. He's with my opponent... Let's give a
> welcome to Macaca, here. Welcome to America and the real
> world of Virginia.*

Sidarth, of Indian ancestry, was born and raised in Fairfax County.
Webb won by a large margin. Allan most likely learned the African racial
slur from his mother, Henrietta "Etty" Allen who had a Jewish upbringing
in Tunisia before moving to the U.S. and concealing the religious aspect
of her identity. In 2006 she told her son, who had not been raised Jewish
that:

> *...she and the senator's father, famed former Redskins coach
> George Allen, had wanted to protect their children from living
> with the fear that she had experienced during World War II.
> Her father, Felix Lumbroso, was imprisoned by the Nazis
> during the occupation of Tunis.*[67]

VIAB's other former board members of note include Tommy P. Baer,
(2007-2010) an immigration and divorce lawyer who escaped Nazi

---

[67] Shear, Michael D., September 22, 2006, *The Chicago Tribune*, "Mom's secret
stirs campaign" https://www.chicagotribune.com/news/ct-xpm-2006-09-22-
0609220110-story.html

Germany. Senator Eric Cantor's wife Diana also served as a Senate appointee from 2005-2008.[68] And the highly influential Anne Holton who served on VIAB's board from 2015-2016 while working as state Secretary of Education. She just happens to be married to Senator Tim Kaine.

---

[68] Full listings of VIAB board members, appointing entity, terms and campaign contributions appear in the appendix.

4.

VIAB MOVES FROM THE GOVERNOR'S OFFICE TO THE STATE LEGISLATURE

We want to clarify to the best of our ability that the Board will appoint ALL staff including the Executive Director, that issue is the impetus for the bill. **VIAB Vice Chairman Charles Lessin**

In 2017 VIAB's leadership desired complete autonomy to choose VIAB's new executive director, rather than have one appointed by the governor. The actions it undertook to achieve that goal revealed the true power of the organization. Early in 2017, the term of Executive Director Ralph Robbins was winding down after nearly 17 years of service. Among his last public appearances was a presentation at a panel called "Strengthening U.S.-Israel Economic Ties" at the annual AIPAC conference in Washington. He spoke[69] alongside Josh Kram of the U.S. Chamber of Commerce and Bill Lane, former executive of Caterpillar. The full topic of the panel discussion was according to the program:

> *Despite the best efforts of the BDS [Boycott, Divestment and Sanctions] movement, US-Israel economic ties continue to deepen. Learn how leading actors enhance the economic relations between the countries and fight back on international efforts to politicize doing business in Israel.*

Robbins founded the American medical Center in Israel, before selling it the year 2000 and joining VIAB as executive director. At the point of his departure from VIAB, countering BDS was a hot topic at board meetings. In July of the previous year, VIAB met in the State Capitol to study an executive order issued by the governor of New York that would halt all state investments or state money flowing into entities engaged in

---

[69] https://vchr.org/viab_foia_responses/03262017.html

Israel boycotts.[70] Making sure its next executive director had an effective anti-BDS profile was key to VIAB's decision to hire Dov Hoch.

2017 INITIATIVE TO APPOINT A NEW EXECUTIVE DIRECTOR

Although under existing statute, VIAB's executive director could only be appointed by the governor, VIAB leadership wanted to move quickly. VIAB posted a job vacancy notice. Robbins informed Todd Haymore, Virginia Secretary of Commerce in the Governor's Office, that VIAB board members Mel Chaskin, Charles Lessin and Jeff Brooks planned to review applications, with interviews taking place on June 17, 2017. A new executive director would be in place by August 1.

Haymore's response was a slap in VIAB's face. On May 23 he told Robbins that, while the governor's office was appreciative of the effort, it was the Governor's sole prerogative to determine among candidates who would be the next executive director of VIAB. As if to add insult to injury, Haymore attached a legal opinion backing up the governor's prerogative citing Virginia code from Deputy Attorney General John Daniel.[71]

The Virginia gubernatorial election was approaching on November 7, 2017. Democratic Party incumbent Terry McAuliffe, who had done so much for VIAB, including traveling with delegations to VIAB projects in Virginia and Israel, was ineligible to run for reelection. It may be that McAuliffe felt the pressure was now off, and that it was time to reassert gubernatorial control over the wildly independent VIAB.

Chairman Mel Chaskin, glumly noted in a July 18, 2017 board meeting that since the executive director was staff, that it was in fact the prerogative of the governor to approve any hire. A "top choice" candidate had already been identified, so now all VIAB had to do was get an official stamp of approval.[72]

But VIAB was losing fans in the Governor's office. Now part of a lame duck administration and personally due to leave by January of 2018, Haymore received a November 14 email with VIAB's annual report sent

---

[70]Robbins, Ralph, March 24, 2017, email "VIAB Board Material for March 30th meeting and information about VIAB and AIPAC" https://vchr.org/viab_foia_responses/07262016.html

[71] Haymore, Todd, Tuesday, May 23, 2017, email "RE: Retirement and Replacement" https://vchr.org/viab_foia_responses/05242017.html

[72] VIAB Board of Director's Meeting, July 18, 2017, "Mel Chaskin reports on AG's decision that the governor should appoint VIAB's executive director," https://vchr.org/viab_foia_responses/07182017.html

from Mel Chaskin's staff at military contractor Vanguard Research. Haymore forwarded it to other staff in the Governor's office noting:

> *I can't argue with the short annual report where they stated they helped create 127 jobs/$426k tax dollars; however, the annual report is likely the most inflated without merit that I've seen in my decade here.*[73]

On November 28, Chaskin told assembled VIAB board members that "while waiting for the Governor's Office to approve VIAB's new Executive Director, we are bringing on a temporary part/time hire our Israel Representative."[74] This "temporary" hire would immediately be contracted for $4,300 per month through February 2018. Chaskin justified the hire on the basis of McAuliffe's deciding that although three candidates had been sent for the governor's approval, VIAB was now leaving the decision to incoming governor Ralph Northam. But major change was afoot.

VIAB "PROPOSES CHANGES" TO ITS CONSTITUTION

Chuck Lessin and Mel Chaskin said they were working on "some proposed changes to the VIAB charter and the possibility of a bill introduction to the Virginia legislature to execute these changes." Already in the month of November, legislation for a major reorganization of VIAB had been pre-filed[75] and was being readied for scrutiny by stakeholders. Chaskin was sure that "whatever bill is proposed will have bipartisan support of the Virginia legislature and we will make sure we have support of the JCRCs."

Chaskin, promised VIAB board members that he would send the new VIAB charter, any proposed changes and a link to the bill for their review. He added:

---

[73] Haymore, Todd, November 15, 2017 email, "Annual Report Memo 2017" https://vchr.org/viab_foia_responses/11152017.html

[74] VIAB Board of Directors Meeting, November 28, 2017, "Discussing Dov Hoch hire and VIAB reorganization." https://vchr.org/viab_foia_responses/11282017.html

[75] A pre-filed bill is submitted for introduction and first reading before the legislative session begins. Pre-filed bills are then introduced on the very first day of the legislative session.

> *Don Ferguson, our representative from the Virginia Attorney
> General's Office, will also assist. The VIAB budget will not
> be affected by any changes to the charter.[76]*

As noted in the previous chapter, it was Ferguson who signed off on
Chuck Lessin's formation of Appalachian Biofuels LLC and receipt of
state funding. VIAB had other victories overcoming conflict of interest
roadblocks in Virginia. The state prohibited any state employee from
accepting money for services performed within the scope of official duties.
Nevertheless, VIAB arranged a $5,000 bonus to outgoing director Ralph
Robbins paid from a tax exempt charity called the Virginia Israel
Foundation. After pushback from the Virginia Conflict of Interest and
Advisory Council, VIAB argued that the check was a "gift" and not a
bonus for work performed. The Virginia Conflict of Interest and Advisory
Council caved and, in the end, accepted the argument.[77]

Representative Tim Hugo pre-filed House Bill 1287 in January of 2018.
Not all of the Federation JCRC's were comfortable with Chaskin and
Lessin's legislative attempt to gain more power and independence as an
authority. Under their proposed legislation, submitted by Hugo, VIAB
was to be renamed the Virginia Israel Advisory Authority. This change
would have moved the new VIAA under the Secretary of Administration
in the executive branch. Fellow authorities would have been entities such
as the "Innovative Technology Authority" and the Virginia Port
Authority.[78] Senator Chap Petersen, who had worked, but failed, to set up
a Virginia Korea Advisory Board in 2014 was approached by a constituent
and consented to filing a companion bill in the Senate (SB15) in January.

On January 12, 2018, Ronald Halber, Executive Director of the Jewish
Community Relations Council of Greater Washington wrote Chaskin, that
moving VIAB out of the Governor's office to become an independent
authority was going too far:

> *As you know, the Executive Committee of our JCRC met on
> Wednesday evening to discuss SB15 [the draft legislation].
> After a lengthy discussion, the Committee decided that it is not
> able to support the bill. Committee members expressed a*

---

[76] VIAB Board of Directors Meeting, November 28, 2017, "Discussing Dov
Hoch hire and VIAB reorganization."
https://vchr.org/viab_foia_responses/11282017.html
[77] Mel Chaskin, VIAB, email, September 7, 2017, "Ralph's Gift."
https://vchr.org/viab_foia_responses/09072017.html
[78] https://www.commonwealth.virginia.gov/va-government/organization-of-
virginia-state-government/

number of serious reservations about the practical effects of establishing VIAB as an independent authority.

Concern [sic] that VIAB will not have the same support from the Governor's office to help in advocating for its budget and will lose existing support and leverage as other agencies and state priorities compete for budget appropriations.

Concern [sic] that the request to grant Virginia's Israel development activities special status, status that no other economic development group enjoys, may draw negative attention to VIAB and result in VIAB's dissolution and absorption into Virginia's greater economic development activities.

Concern about what accountability measure will be put in place other than issuance of an annual report.

We understand that you and Chuck have legitimate concerns related to VIAB's current structure and the difficulty in hiring an executive director, but we do not believe that this bill provides the appropriate remedy. We would be open to working on a solution together.[79]

But Ralph Robbins, writing near simultaneously as VIAB Executive Director Emeritus, told Delegates Tim Hugo and Chap Petersen that the governor's delays on rubber stamping VIAB's inside candidate was unprecedented and more than warranted VIAB becoming an independent authority.[80]

VIAB board member Will Franks, a gubernatorial appointee from Henrico serving from 2015-2018 thought the legislation was flawed. There was no requirement the governor provide office space. The bill said the authority would henceforth control staff, but Frank questioned whether a $215,184 budget would cover the expense.[81]

---

[79] Ronald Halber, Executive Director of the Jewish Community Relations Council of Greater Washington, email, January 12, 2018, https://vchr.org/viab_foia_responses/01122018.html

[80] Ralph Robbins, Executive Director Emeritus, VIAB, letter to Tim Hugo and Chap Petersen, January 14, 2018 https://vchr.org/viab_foia_responses/01142018.html

[81] Frank, Will, VIAB board member, January 28, 2018 email to Mel Chaskin about the VIAB Charter Legislation, copied to over 30 VIAB board members, Federation and JCRC community members. https://vchr.org/viab_foia_responses/01282018.html

Charles Lessin worked with Amigo Wade of the Division of Legislative Services and outside lobbyist Matthew Benka of MDB Strategies to put House Bill (1297) into better shape. Matt Benka was a logical choice and probably did the lobbying work for free. That is because he was also the paid lobbyist for Caden Energix, Oran Safety Glass, and UBQ as well as many of Lessin's gambling interests.[82] But the House bill was also highly flawed in VIAB's view. It had the legislature's Joint Rules Committee appointing VIAB's executive director.[83] On February 7, Lessin gruffly insisted that:

> *We want to clarify to the best of our ability that the Board will appoint ALL staff including the Executive Director, that issue is the impetus for the bill. Can we add to line 41, a sentence that reads; All Staff members shall be appointed by the board.*

But other flaws were found in the legislation. Lauren Schmitt, outgoing Deputy Legislative Director in the governor's office advised lobbyist Matt Benka and a staffer for Delegate Tim Hugo that:

> *…the funds budgeted for the Board in the Executive Department have to be transferred to the legislative Department…not sure how it works at this point in the process, but we'll need to move quickly…can Delegate Hugo talk to Chairman Jones and find out the appropriate next steps?[84]*

On February 27, Matt Benka sounded an alarm bell, saying:

> *…unfortunately, there has been a bit of confusion on VIAB issues in the Senate. Had a long conversation with Senator [Frank] Ruff this afternoon, Hugo and Senate staff to try to get everyone back on the same page.[85]*

Senator Ryan McDougle appeared to have "gone rogue" by issuing a February 28 substitute amendment on 1297 which would have reorganized

---

[82] Benka, Matthew D., lobbyist profile by the Virginia Public Access Project
https://www.vpap.org/lobbying/lobbyist/93577-matthew-d-benka/

[83] HB 1297 Virginia-Israel Advisory Board; reorganizes as Virginia-Israel Advisory Authority, 2018 legislative session, passed
https://lis.virginia.gov/cgi-bin/legp604.exe?181+sum+HB1297

[84] Schmitt, Lauren, email to Matthew Benka and Dean Goodson, February 11, 2018. https://vchr.org/viab_foia_responses/02112018.html

[85] Benka, Matthew, email to Lauren Schmitt copied to Mel Chaskin and Charles Lessin, February 27, 2018.
https://vchr.org/viab_foia_responses/02272018.html

VIAB under the Virginia Economic Development Partnership, which would have had the power to designate VIAB's executive director "from existing authority staff."[86] In other words, the exact opposite of what VIAB was attempting to achieve. Chap Petersen, who had sponsored SB15, had already been approached by yet another constituent, and was convinced to ask to strike his own Senate bill (SB15) on January 9.

HOUSE BILL 1297

Somehow, McDougle was corralled back into VIAB's corner. Kim Clark of Vanguard Research on March 14 forwarded a message from Mel Chaskin that VIAB had gotten what it wanted in passage of modified House Bill 1297.[87] The governor's appointees to VIAB's board were reduced to only five, with House and Senate appointing ten each. Jewish federations could appoint four board members (that had to live in Virginia) while the Secretary of Commerce and Education could appoint two board members. Chaskin was ecstatic it squeezed through:

> *We were the very last action of both the house and senate. They both waited 45 minutes to adjourn! Hugo and McDougle did us a huge favor by doing this.*[88]

On March 19, Matt Benka also announced passage of a modified House Bill 1297 that moved VIAB (and its budgeted $215,000 in funding) out of the governor's office and invited legislators to meet with Chaskin, and Lessin to familiarize themselves with VIAB initiatives. Lauren Schmitt declined invitations to celebrate VIAB's victory and on May 25, tendered her resignation to leave the office of the governor for the lobbying firm Commonwealth Strategy Group. Before her scheduled departure, Mel Chaskin, had one final favor to ask of his friend in the governor's office:

> *I know you are leaving, but I would like to ask you to try and get someone from the Secretary of Commerce and Trade to send the approval for Dov's trip in the Middle of May. You told me*

---

[86] House Bill No. 1297 Amendment in the Nature of a Substitute, 2018 session http://lis.virginia.gov/cgi-bin/legp604.exe?181+ful+HB1297S1

[87] Chaskin, Mel, message in a forwarded email to VIAB members, March 14, 2018 https://vchr.org/viab_foia_responses/03142018.html

[88] Chaskin, Mel, message in a forwarded email to VIAB members, March 14, 2018 https://vchr.org/viab_foia_responses/03142018.htmlhttps://vchr.org/viab_foia_responses/03142018.html

it was approved but Dennis Johnson [Fiscal Director of the Commonwealth of Virginia] has not been told. Good luck in your new job.[89]

Dov Hoch, traveling through Virginia via Israel, could now finally, nearly a year later than planned, assume his fulltime position as VIAB's executive director.

VIAB's 2018 reconstitution under the legislature depended on concentrated pressure exerted by Jewish federations. This much was admitted in 2019 by Nathan Shor, past president of the Jewish Community Federation of Richmond (and VIAB director 2016-2018) in a joint event with Dov Hoch:

> *The bigger question is here, because we do change governors for sure every 4 years. So, by changing administrations we have got agencies where the governor and the staff don't understand us, this is not a good rapport. We did have that battle when Ralph retired. VIAB won that battle with the help of all the Federations of Jews in the community. But, they wanted to make us state appointees...It would have been a worthless job at that point, because then you're turning over every four years, and then why point out a big donor who may have no connection to Israel, you have got to have this connection, you've got to be able to pick up the phone like Ralph did, like Dov does, to get to those right decision makers. So, more importantly, when we changed administrations here, VIAB has no concern whether we're going to change executive directors.[90]*

From the outside, Dov Hoch, who was temporarily put on salary, appears all along to have been the inside candidate mostly because he was committed to addressing outgoing Executive Director Ralph Robbin's concerns about the BDS movement.

The BDS movement emerged from a bloody—and lopsided in terms of casualties— wave of violence between Palestinians and Israel's military in 2002. A group of Palestinian academics published a call for boycott the next year and in 2004 a group called the Palestinian Academic and Cultural Boycott of Israel put out its formal appeal. Signatories had limited access

---

[89] Chaskin, Mel, email to Lauren Schmitt, May 27, 2018.
https://vchr.org/viab_foia_responses/05272018.html

[90] Hoch, Dov, "What VIAB Does and How it Benefits Virginia," speech at the Weinstein Jewish Community Center, Richmond, VA, April 4, 2019. Introduction and remarks by former president of the Jewish Federation of Richmond Nathan Shor

to books and were under severe Israeli travel restrictions. Their call for action charged that the Israeli occupation had so severely curtailed the academic freedom of Palestinian colleges and universities that calling for a global censure against Israel on their behalf was the only nonviolent means to confront injustice.

Responding to a 2012 BDS conference at the University of Pennsylvania, Dov Hoch (a 1986 graduate and then president of the Penn Club of Israel) issued a mocking, boastful call for pro-Palestinian attendees to avail themselves of massive subsidies from the private and public sector and build something, rather than calling attention to Israeli's treatment of Palestinians:

> *So perhaps it might make sense to change the BDS mindset to one of investment and genuine nation-building activities. If BDS's conviction remain one of divestment; one of burning your neighbor's house despite the fact you live in connected structures and all-the-more linked economies, then to be most effective conference goers should stop using Microsoft and Google products as well; both companies have several research and development centers in Israel, as do most cellular handset manufacturers. And please throw out your iPhones — Apple just bought an Israeli company.[91]*

But although VIAB mostly doesn't publicly mention it, a major reason behind its drive to partner Israeli and U.S. companies within the United States and beyond is the threat posed by the Boycott Divestment and Sanctions movement. By licensing technology, operating secret shell companies where only a few insiders know the beneficial owners, and joint venturing with larger U.S. companies, Israeli companies can make it more difficult for activists to target them to change the Israeli government's behavior. It is the reason Dov Hoch has returned to the United States to work in the Pocahontas building in Richmond. But anti-BDS work in Virginia had already begun before his arrival.

In March of 2016[92] the Virginia General Assembly passed resolution HJ 177 the "anti-Israel boycott, Divestment and Sanctions (BDS) Condemnation" which claimed that the BDS movement was hampering peace and preventing negotiations while claiming boycotts were not a legitimate accountability tactic. BDS by that time had grown

---

[91] Hoch, Dov, February 2, 2012, "Why we should invest, not divest," *The Daily Pennsylvanian,* https://www.thedp.com/article/2012/02/4f28ebda5c0f0

[92] HJ 177 Anti-Israel Boycott, Divestment, and Sanctions (BDS); condemnation, 2016 Virginia legislative session, passed https://lis.virginia.gov/cgi-bin/legp604.exe?161+sum+HJ177

into a call for economically boycotting Israel over its human rights record, more specifically the military occupation of Palestinian territories and mistreatment of Palestinians.

VIAB's annual budget is only a couple hundred thousand per year. It therefore does not directly provide tax holidays, economic development grants, or subsidize job training for Israeli companies all while fighting BDS. However, VIAB does work to identify, develop and steer such corporate subsidies to Israeli companies by lobbying fellow state agencies and the state legislature from within government. We examine its tactics in the chapters about specific companies VIAB either brought, or is bringing, to Virginia.

5.

U.S. AID TO ISRAEL AND SUBSIDIES FOR ISRAELI MILITARY CONTRACTORS

I'm very familiar with the Israeli military. And I can go anywhere I wanted. But had I not represented a government, they would [have] said, 'Great strategy. You want to help us execute it.' But they would not have come here. . . **Dov Hoch, Executive Director of the Virginia Israel Advisory Board**[93]

Israel has long been the leading recipient of U.S. foreign assistance. It is impossible to say precisely how much Israel receives. The Congressional Research Service publishes an annual report with top line numbers and significant details about U.S. aid. By 2020, cumulative inflation adjusted aid will reach $282.4 billion.

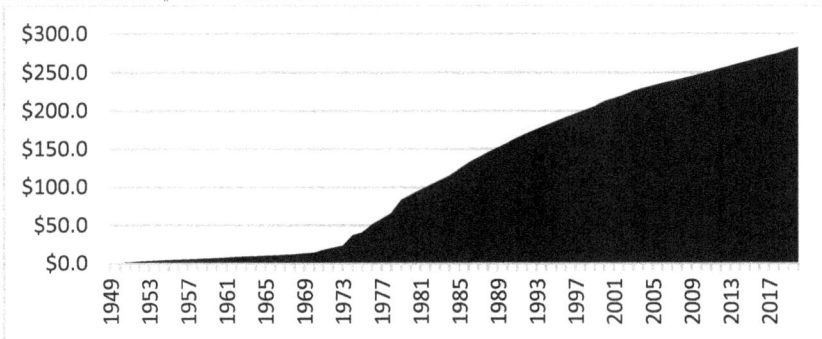

7 CUMULATIVE INFLATION ADJUSTED UNCLASSIFIED U.S. FOREIGN AID TO ISRAEL ($ BILLION)[94]

---

[93] Dov, Hoch, "What VIAB Does and How it Benefits Virginia," speech at the Weinstein Jewish Community Center, Richmond, VA, April 4, 2019. Introduction and remarks by former president of the Jewish Federation of Richmond Nathan Shor

[94] Sharp, Jeremy, "U.S. Foreign Aid to Israel," Congressional Research Service series of reports, inflation adjusted by the author.

Excluded from that figure is any hard or estimated figure for U.S. intelligence aid to Israel, from the so-called "black budget." But such aid exists, as verified by President Barack Obama in a speech at American University on August 5, 2015. He said:

> ...But the fact is, partly due to American military and intelligence assistance, which my administration has provided at unprecedented levels, Israel can defend itself against any conventional danger—whether from Iran directly or from its proxies.[95]

The CRS report, which is meant to inform Congress and not the public, used to report that Americans were broadly supportive of such aid. For example, in 2011, report author Jeremy Sharp wrote that:

> Though aid to Israel has both supporters and detractors, overall U.S. public support for Israel remains strong. According to a February 2011 Gallup poll that measured Americans' sympathies toward the disputants in the Israeli-Palestinian conflict, a near record-high 63% said their sympathies lie more with the Israelis.[96]

Using Gallup results as a proxy was necessary, explained the CRS report author because, "There is less specific public polling data on support for aid to Israel."

However, there were two major problems with Sharp's claims. The first was that Gallup's polls were so flawed that it was forced to admit in 2019 that the way it asked questions "primed" respondents to give artificially high "sympathy for Israel" responses.[97] Jeffrey M. Jones at Gallup even wrote in "Survey Context Effects on Middle East Sympathies" that:

> ...the priming effect of asking country favorability appears to push people toward sympathizing with Israel rather than expressing no opinion (or not taking a side). The theory is that after respondents answer some questions on international

---

[95] Remarks by the President on the Iran Nuclear Deal, American University, August 5, 2015, Whitehouse.gov

[96] Sharp, Jeremy, "U.S. Foreign Aid to Israel," Congressional Research Service series of reports, 2012 http://dev.journalistsresource.org/wp-content/uploads/2012/04/Military-Aid-to-Israel.pdf

[97] Jones, Jeffrey M., Gallup "Survey Context Effects on Middle East Sympathies" March 28, 2019 https://news.gallup.com/opinion/methodology/248078/survey-context-effects-middle-east-sympathies.aspx

*affairs, they may become more focused on the topic and more
comfortable expressing opinions (including weakly held ones) in
response to subsequent questions on that same topic.*

Gallup's admission meant, given its use of the same methodologies and
questions year after year, that three decades of sympathy polls overstated
popular sympathy for Israel. Israel affinity organizations, which invariably
amplified Gallup's survey releases every year, have been slow to remove
such data from their websites.

The other claims, that there is so little public opinion polling about U.S.
support for aid to Israel as to be not worth reporting is also false. Since
U.S. aid to Israel is such a large percentage of the aid budget, it is worth
specifically polling year after year. Representative polls conducted for
more than a half decade through Google Consumer Surveys reveal strong
and growing popular opposition to U.S. aid for Israel.[98]

Another problem with U.S. aid to Israel is that it is made on the
premise that it helps maintain Israel's "qualitative military edge," defined
as the technological, tactical, and other advantages that allow it to deter
numerically superior adversaries. Absent from that discussion is any
realistic factoring in of Israel's nuclear weapons arsenal. Since Israel has
nuclear weapons, why should the U.S. continually deliver massive supplies
of conventional use weapons and duel use platforms, such as jet fighters,
that Israel can use to deliver nuclear weapons? This question has never
satisfactorily been answered by Israel's supporters or U.S. officials.

A final issue is the legal ban on U.S. foreign aid to clandestine nuclear
weapons states. Under the Symington and Glenn amendments now
incorporated into the Arms Export Control Act, no U.S. president
knowing about Israel's nukes is supposed to approve aid transfers, absent
specifically issued waivers. Rather than comply with the law, presidents
pretend they don't know Israel has nukes and issue agency wide gag orders
threatening any government employee who talks about it.

MEMORANDUM OF UNDERSTANDING

With U.S. military spending surging from $686 billion in 2019 to over
$710 billion in 2020, Israeli companies are eager to participate in the
windfall. As part of that strategy, they may also be attempting to skirt
Obama-era "buy American" restrictions on U.S. foreign aid to Israel by
establishing subsidiaries in Virginia or partnering with major U.S. arms
manufacturers and military service providers.

---

[98] IRmep Polls: https://IRmep.org/polls/

On September 14, 2016, the United States and Israel signed a "memorandum of understanding" (MOU) pledging $38 billion in "security assistance" to Israel over ten years. The agreement replaced a similar $31 billion ten year MOU signed by the George W. Bush administration. "Buy American" provisions in the ten-year allotment required most of the foreign aid to Israel must be spent on U.S. military contractors rather than within Israel on Israeli military contractors. In an official statement, the Obama White House claimed:

> *Off shore Procurement (the arrangement under the current MOU through which Israel has been uniquely permitted to spend 26.3 percent of its annual FMF package within Israel on non-U.S. products) and Israel's use of FMF funds to purchase fuel — means that Israel will spend more funding, as much as $1.2 billion per year, on the advanced military capabilities that only the United States can provide. The acquisition of additional U.S.-produced capabilities and technology provide the best means to ensure Israel preserves its Qualitative Military Edge (QME).*

The MOU is silent on whether U.S. based wholly owned subsidiaries of Israeli military contractors, such as IAI North America and Elbit Systems of America, count as "Israeli" or "U.S." vendors. Israelis and their U.S. boosters such as VIAB presume that all they have to do to recapture "their share" of the spending is to set up shop in Virginia. Dov Hoch is on record telling audiences that U.S. taxpayer funded aid formerly spent on Israeli military contractors is essentially money "coming from Israel:"

> *Until now, a quarter of that was brought to Israel in the form of moneys that could be bought, used and applied in Israel in shekels, it didn't have to be, "buy America", you know, buy a fighter jet. . . . A billion dollars could be a good thing, used in Israel and by Israeli manufacturers. Obama terminated that. But we have a billion dollars in contracts, captive contracts, that Israeli companies are currently holding that need to be manufactured in US. This is what I do day and night, day and night. I said to the Israeli Army, the unit that does export and takes care of these things, I said, you come to Virginia, it's right near the ecosystem where everybody sells to the US Army. It's got the manufacturing capacity. I don't know if you know this, Lockheed Martin, they're in Maryland. Northrop Grumman is in Virginia. General Dynamics is headquartered in Virginia. I told the Israeli army, if you come here, I will find you partners. I'm not going to build businesses. We'll take those*

> *Israeli companies; we'll bring them here; we'll find them a*
> *Virginia manufacturing partner. I'll tell the Virginians we*
> *have a captive contract up to a billion dollars coming from*
> *Israel.*[99]

But what support does VIAB give to Israeli companies trying to get in on the bonanza? A great deal, it turns out. VIAB can either directly or indirectly compensate former high-ranking U.S. officers to work on creating opportunities for Israeli military contractors. Nathan Shor trumpeted this capability in the context of a spring 2019 matchmaking event hosted in Tysons Corner bringing together 70 businesspeople and government officials.[100]

> *This is an extraordinary event. Three days for naval related*
> *military technologies in the Hampton Roads footprint. We have*
> *three admirals in that area working with us and for us to do*
> *that project. We have a half time, third time employee down in*
> *that area who is like an assistant.*[101]

VIAB's biggest intellectual legacy on the military contracting front is clearly Mel Chaskin. Like Charles Lessin, his real bio and activities are infinitely more revealing than what appears on the VIAB website.

MEL CHASKIN AND VANGUARD RESEARCH

Mel Chaskin was born in New York City and got his start as a software engineer with Grumman in the 1960's when the company was flush with contracts for the Apollo moon landing program. He served as a system flight test pilot supporting the U.S. Air Force with military contractor Lear Siegler, Inc and entered government civil service in 1971. He managed U.S. Air Force long range navigation, space communications and

---

[99] Hoch, Dov, "What VIAB Does and How it Benefits Virginia," speech at the Weinstein Jewish Community Center, Richmond, VA, April 4, 2019. Introduction and remarks by former president of the Jewish Federation of Richmond Nathan Shor

[100] Virginia-Israel defense contractor event held in Tysons, April 5, 2019, *The Fairfax County Times,* http://www.fairfaxtimes.com/articles/virginia-israel-defense-contractor-event-held-in-tysons/article_750c5fdc-57eb-11e9-99e4-ebb69108b232.html

[101] Shore, Nathan, remarks by former president of the Jewish Federation of Richmond, "What VIAB Does and How it Benefits Virginia," speech at the Weinstein Jewish Community Center, Richmond, VA, April 4, 2019. introducing Dov Hoch

experimental satellite programs, as well as command and control systems. Chaskin rose through the civilian ranks to a position supporting the Assistant Secretary of Defense.

In 1981 Chaskin left government service and in March of 1984 founded his own military contracting company Vanguard Research Incorporated. By August of that year, Vanguard signed its first contract for $34,000.

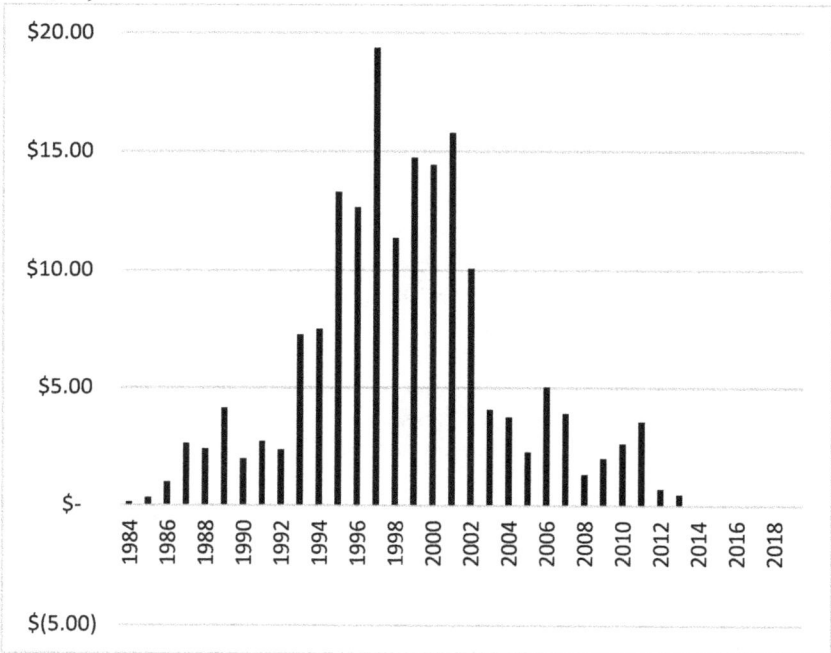

8 VANGUARD RESEARCH U.S. GOVERNMENT MILITARY CONTRACTS 1984-2019 ($ U.S. MILLION)[102]

Business gathered steam as Vanguard contracted to perform special studies and analysis with the U.S. Army and Air Force. By the late 1980s, as the Reagan administration's Strategic Defense Initiative "Star Wars" missile defense was launched, Vanguard's contracts shifted into systems engineering and R&D on missile and space systems. By the end of the 1980's Vanguard picked up work directly with the Missile Defense Agency, which had its origins in Star Wars.

Vanguard's peak contracting year, by total awards, was the year 2001 when it won almost $16 million in contracts. The firm's business in relatively small sequential contracts, averaging less than a quarter million

---

[102] Federal Procurement Data System, consulted September 25, 2019
https://www.fpds.gov

dollars, was steady. What distinguished a good year from a bad one was the number of contracts. The late 1990s and early aughts were great because Vanguard was handling more than 50 contracts per year. Business began winding down as average contracts won by Vanguard dropped below 20 per year.

Through 2019, Vanguard Research was the recipient of just under $174 million in contracts. Mel Chaskin's experience and insight into the world of military contracting and steady business in small contracts would serve VIAB well with the year 2006 Virginia debut of a bulletproof glass maker founded at an obscure Israeli kibbutz in 1979.

6.
SHAM MILITARY CONTRACTING AT ORAN SAFETY GLASS

We even have a kibbutz that brought a company here to Emporia. If you know this Oran Safety Glass (OSG) they make all bullet-proof glass for the principal battle tank for the U.S. army, the Abrams battle tank. A little baby kibbutz right near Jerusalem. They built a facility here ten years ago. They doubled the capacity two times. Just recently increased the workforce by 50%. Since they came here, they exposed themselves to the civilian market, and they are selling now basically bullet-proof glass to Caterpillar tractors and Bombardier train engines in Canada and they're very, very successful here. **Dov Hoch, VIAB Executive Director**

In presentations before Israeli business leaders, Dov Hoch emphasizes the unique funding possibilities available in Virginia courtesy of the massive settlement won in court against tobacco companies and a specialized state fund designed to revitalize former coal producing regions. No VIAB project is more exemplary of "multiple bites of the apple" than Oran Safety Glass repeatedly tapping multiple levels of funding and loan guarantees to build its U.S. military contracting business.

The manufacture and sale of "transparent armor" to the Department of Defense to protect personnel operating military vehicles has long been a mature industry in the United States. When the Department of Defense issued a series of U.S. Army contracts for windows to be installed in "mine-resistant ambush-protected" all-terrain vehicles known as "MRAPs" in 2014, it wasn't seeking cutting-edge, technological advances. Rather, it wanted competent contractors to bid (through "source approval requests", or SARS) on making transparent armor according to a government-developed and owned "secret recipe." This item was so routinely procured, inventoried and installed that it had its own "stock number."

For the newly opened Israeli subsidiary Oran Safety Glass in Greensville County, there were only two major challenges it would face if it won competitive bidding for the contracts. The first was that the U.S. government owned not only the "recipe" but also specifications about the specific threats against which the glass would protect, and the ballistic testing procedures for the glass. All were U.S. government classified information at the SECRET level. Oran Safety Glass in 2014 did not have an officially designated "facility clearance" for handling such classified information. It also had no way to efficiently procure the materials needed to produce transparent armor required in the specifications in the government's "secret recipe."

Neither of those obstacles prevented OSG from bidding on and lowballing U.S. industry leaders. OSG won five contracts between October 2014 and 2015.

ORAN SUBMITS FRAUDULENT BIDS ON U.S. GOVERNMENT CONTRACTS

In 2015, one of those industry leaders, Schott Government Services, contacted the Army and requested production control ballistics testing of OSG's shipments. The Army soon discovered that most of the OSG manufactured armor was "out of specification." Alarmed, the Army formally notified OSG that such products manufactured by means other than its own "recipe" would be considered unauthorized and non-compliant.

OSG responded that it was producing a different recipe after it developed internal concerns about the availability and quality of M-ATV[103] compliant raw materials. OSG argued that after performing tests on its own "recipe" it found that its already-delivered, out-of-spec products produced out of compliance with the contracts "did not affect performance" and that it had even submitted its own recipe to the Army as a source approval request (SAR) for future sales.

The U.S. Army was placed under enormous pressure by OSG's actions. Some of OSG's products had already been installed on vehicles and any supply chain issues would delay its supply lines. The product was desperately needed. That much is known with certainty. What is not known is whether OSG rallied any friends within Congress, the Department of Defense, or elsewhere to cut a deal with the buyer. What is certain is that a sweetheart deal was indeed made.

On June 4, 2015 the U.S. Army approved OSG's new recipe, which transcended the pressing problem of the already received and installed transparent glass armor. The Army didn't cancel any of OSG's contracts. However, on June 24, 2015 it ordered any future OSG deliveries would have to comply with the original U.S. government owned "secret recipe"

---

[103] The Oshkosh M-ATV is a Mine Resistant Ambush Protected (MRAP) vehicle developed by the Oshkosh Corporation for the MRAP

specified in the contract. It also ordered OSG to make cash and in-kind payments to cover additional government costs incurred for handling and processing "nonconforming goods previously delivered." But it allowed OSG to extend delivery times on "all outstanding deliveries."

OSG's competitors were livid, and one even sued over the contract.[104] But the litigant could not convince the presiding judge that there was any prejudice in the actual issuance of the contract. The legal standard for prejudice is establishing that if it had not been for a procurement process error, they could have won the contract. Since they were—unlike OSG— not low-balling and intending to manufacture and deliver non-compliant products, their prices were so high that the legal standard intended to prevent prejudicial awards could not protect them. As discussed later, it is possible that a False Claims Act lawsuit could have remedied the situation, but OSG, like other VIAB companies operating across Virginia, is an extremely unlikely place for such lawsuits ever to be filed.

ORAN'S PENTAGON CONTRACTS

The fact that particular contracts are for MRAPs is a secret. So, the five contracts cannot be identified from within publicly accessible listings of payments that have exact dollar amounts related to contracts awarded to OSG. However, military contract databases do reveal that in 2016, in an uncharacteristic move, OSG repaid the U.S. government $4.7 million. It is not known if any American military personnel who's lives depended on non-compliant OSG armor, ever paid the ultimate price over the contracting malfeasance.

---

[104] SCHOTT GOVERNMENT SERVICES, LLC, Plaintiff, v. THE UNITED STATES, Defendant, ORAN SAFETY GLASS, INC.,
https://scholar.google.com/scholar_case?case=11340217780044701718&q= schott+government+services+vs+oran+safety+glass&hl=en&as_sdt=20006 #r[1]

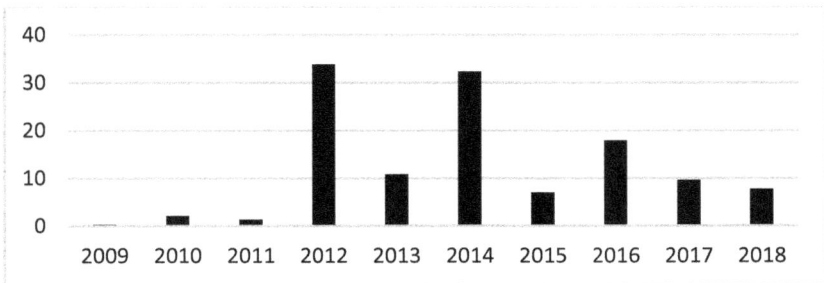

40									
30									
20									
10									
0									
2009	2010	2011	2012	2013	2014	2015	2016	2017	2018

9 YEARLY OSG REVENUE FROM U.S. GOVERNMENT MILITARY CONTRACTS 2009-2018 ($ MILLION)[105]

From the perspective of U.S. taxpayers, there are a number of problems with the way OSG does business that are unique to its operations as not only an Israeli company, but an Israeli military contractor.

The first is OSG's ability to, without being cleared to access or store U.S. government classified information, bid on contracts that require and necessitate conferring that status upon the successful bidder. This risk has produced negative outcomes in the past. The Nuclear Materials and Equipment Corporation, which also obtained and stored classified U.S. government information in its Apollo, PA nuclear materials processing site, invited top Israeli spies into its plant facilities, creating a conundrum for regulators concerned about its improbably high "losses" of weapons-grade nuclear material. NUMEC also employed an Israeli scientist to learn how to handle plutonium, long before Israel was able to produce it at its nuclear weapons production facilities. This employee was not in any way formally cleared by U.S. regulators to be working on such delicate matters.

Israel's theft and use of U.S. classified and proprietary technologies, including technology diversions to China, are well documented and even legendary. It is improbable to assume that any of the innovative processes contained in the U.S. "secret recipe" did not ultimately make their way back to OSG headquarters in Israel and then onward to parts unknown.

Finally, the corporate hierarchy and culture at OSG subverts the primary tool preventing fraud in U.S. government contracting, the False Claims Act. The federal statute was originally enacted in response to defense contractor fraud during the American Civil War. Today, it allows corporate insiders to file suits on behalf of the government against companies that defrauded U.S. government agencies. Filed under seal, if

---

[105] Federal Procurement Data System – Next Generation, http://Pfds.gov consulted on 9/27/2019

the Department of Justice joins the action, a plaintiff "whistleblower" can sue and receive a portion of any funds recovered by the government. This law is not only applied in instances of military contract fraud. In 2012 pollster Gallup was charged under the False Claims Act over a failed U.S. Mint contract to launch $4 billion worth of dollar denominated coins. Gallup paid $10.5 million in fines for overbilled, faulty polling work provided to the U.S. Department of Treasury and other government agencies.

At OSG, as with many other VIAB projects, top management consists of Israeli and prominent American Jews not just committed to OSG's business objectives, but commitment to grow the business as an expression of their support for Israel. They would be subjected to extreme and unusual pressure in a False Claims Act scenario. Consider what happened to American journalist Leonard Fein, editor of the liberal Jewish magazine *Moment*, after he expressed—in the eyes of Israelis—disloyalty through his actions.

In 1980 Fein organized a group of 56 prominent American Jews to sign a letter saying Israeli Prime Minister Menachem Begin was lying about Israel's plans for expanding illegal settlements. He described what happened:

> *I was fingered as the organizer of this little movement. Some two years later, I was interviewed in Israel by the Jerusalem Post. And the Post said, "What gives you the right to criticize Israeli policy?" I said, "Look when Begin comes back from his visits to America and gets off the plane, he always says, 'I have great news, the American Jewish community is 100 percent behind us.' And if he's going to say that, I'm going to correct him, because it simply is not so."*
>
> *The reporter from the Post [asked] "are you calling Begin a liar?" I said, "Use whatever word you want, that's all I have to say." The next day, front page, Jerusalem Post, "American Professor calls Begin a liar." And my roof fell in. I depended on wealthy liberal Jews to support Moment magazine. Money was withdrawn right and left from its support...[106]*

Fein's story could be retold by hundreds, if not thousands, of other conscientious American Jews standing up in a way perceived as harmful to Israel. Within many Jewish circles, particularly those most dedicated to

---

[106] Weiss, Philip, October 3, 2013, "When Leonard Fein criticized right winger Menachem Begin– 'the roof fell in'" Mondoweiss https://mondoweiss.net/2013/10/criticized-rightwinger-menachem/

Israel, a "Shonda" is doing something shameful that is publicly witnessed by non-Jews. This, in turn is said to bring shame on all Jews in general because, particularly as Zionists tend to claim, all Jews are held accountable for "the worst deeds of the worst among us." Or, in other words, fellow Americans are just so bigoted that they automatically project the bad actions of individuals, small groups or organizations and the identity of an entire class of Americans.

What if OSG did bid on the MRAP contract, knowing full well that it could not procure the U.S. government's "secret recipe" compliant materials? What if an Israeli manager at the company, or Jewish American working in management, then filed a False Claims Act lawsuit alleging the company knowingly low-balled its bid in order to win the contract, knowing full well that it had no intention of complying with its terms?

Even after prevailing in court, where would the employee go? Certainly not to Israel. If he or she were to remain in the U.S., the whistle blower could instantly lose access to his immediate establishment pro-Israel community. He or she would also probably spend the rest of his days looking over his back, like Victor Ostrovsky, a former Mossad officer who wrote two bestselling nonfiction books exposing the agency's practices, and who now quietly runs an art gallery somewhere in the West.

STATE GOVERNMENT FUNDING FOR ORAN

Unexplored in news media accounts about Oran are any meticulous compilations of precisely how much taxpayer funded and other government aid the Israeli company has soaked up thanks to VIAB. The funding comes in from multiple levels. That is VIAB strategy:

> *The place where you can make a difference, is on the local level. And this is something most Israeli companies don't understand. Here [in Israel] we have one level of government, for all practical purposes. On the U.S. side, you've got states, counties, cities, and even neighborhoods. So that's where the negotiation comes to play.* **Sherwin Pomerantz, Founding Chairperson, American State Offices Association, speaking alongside Dov Hoch, executive director VIAB**[107]

---

[107] Hoch, Dov and Pomerantz, Sherwin, "US Financial Incentives for Israeli Companies" Presentation at the Israel American Business Summit, May 29, 2019

Most news reports about Oran portray the opposite of reality. One year 2019 report, from the *Area Development Online* news organization runs the headline, "Oran Safety Glass Expands Greensville County, Virginia, Manufacturing Complex."[108] A far more accurate headline would have been, "Greensville County Expands Oran Safety Glass Complex." Initially VIAB and Oran played every angle to squeeze millions in funding out of the state and county, all so Oran could be well-positioned to submit fraudulent bids for U.S. military contracts. Oran is now one of VIAB's most cherished projects, and is prominently featured in its promotional materials, as mentioned in VIAB meeting minutes:

> We are marketing ourselves in Israel, [and] created a brochure. Leveraging United Airlines direct flight[s]. Using mass media organizations. We are focused on doing a campaign geared to the Kibbutz industry. A lot of innovation in water and technology has come from that niche (i.e. Drip Irrigation and desalinization). We have one kibbutz business that came to Virginia, Oran Safety Glass in Emporia, currently employing 150 people. They sell their glass to the military and Caterpillar tractor, they sell back to Israel through foreign military funding, and to the civilian market. A tiny Kibbutz company has expanded exponentially. Sometimes it takes a known person that is trusted to guide these small companies to take interest in the US.[109]

Oran did indeed start out as the main industry of the Tzubga kibbutz located in the Judean Hills of central Israel. Since its founding in 1979, it grew to become Israel's leading manufacturer of "transparent armor." It markets its products for use in "military, paramilitary and civilian" applications, with the latter concentrated in projectile resistant train and bus windshields, though it is entering glass digital displays to project information in public transportation settings.[110] And as noted, the U.S. Department of Defense does procure OSG products within what the

---

[108] "Oran Safety Glass Expands Greensville County, Virginia, Manufacturing Complex" Area Development News Desk, September 8, 2017, https://www.areadevelopment.com/newsItems/9-8-2017/oran-safety-glass-manufacturing-operation-greensville-county-virginia.shtml

[109] VIAB Meeting minutes, November 27, 2018 p3

[110] Oran Safety Glass, Company Movie, November 5, 2014. https://www.youtube.com/watch?v=Z01raca4-1g

Pentagon designates as the "Military Armored Vehicle, Tank, And Tank Component Manufacturing" sector. But how much of a boost did access to the U.S. government owned "secret recipe" give to Oran? With its penchant for output substitution, is any of the civilian product sold for freight trains and bus windshields derived from that secret formula? What about foreign military sales based on the formula from OSG in Israel?

Oran has received mammoth ongoing support in Virginia delivered in three phases. The first, for Oran to set up operations in Virginia, and two expansion phases as defense contracts poured in. In July of 2006 a performance agreement was executed between Oran, the Virginia Economic Development Partnership, the Tobacco Commission and Greensville County. The parties agreed that in exchange for government support OSG would make a $4.1 million capital investment to start production in Virginia and create 45 new jobs within 30 months.

In 2007 the Greensville County Industrial Development Authority leased five and a third acres of land and an 82,800 square foot industrial building for ten years to OSG.[111] The County obtained grants to perform a nearly $600,000 upgrade to the facility, including two separate Tobacco Commission grants in the amounts of $100,000 and $125,000, a $50,000 Emporia/Greensville Industrial Development Corporate grant, as well as $125,000 from the Governor's Opportunity Fund. The project also applied for a Virginia Department of Housing and Community Development "Virginia Enterprise Zone Real Property Improvement Grant" of $125,000.

Greensville County even agreed to go into debt to bring in OSG by securing a loan for $400,000 from the Virginia Small Business Finance Authority to cover any "Phase I" cost shortfalls. There were cascading effects. Other entities such as the Mecklenburg Electric Cooperative also agreed to go into debt by up to $400,000 to build out infrastructure necessary to supply electricity to OSG. The county also waived water and sewer connection fees in the amount of $20,000 and $4,300 in building permitting fees. The government parties also showered another quarter million dollars of "job creation grants," "training and recruitment incentive grants" and free classroom space for "pre-employment testing and training" to assist in the creation of a workforce for OSG.

---

[111] On December 17, 2017, the Greensville County Industrial Development Authority sold the facility, which it carried on its books as a $1,140,000 asset to Oran Safety Glass for a price equivalent to the outstanding loan balance on the property, or $436,644. See https://IsraelLobby.org/Oran for details.

2007 Location

Facilities upgrade grants	Amount
Tobacco Region Opportunity Fund Grant	$ 100,000
Tobacco Region Opportunity Fund Grant	$ 125,000
Governor's Opportunity Fund - VEDP	$ 125,000
Job creation and Training and Recruitment	$ 250,000
Dept of Housing and Community Development Block Grant	$ 125,000
Phase 1 Loans - Greensville County	
Virginia Small Business Finance Authority	$ 400,000
Mecklenburg Electric Cooperative Loans	
Debt to build electricity connectivity to plant	$ 400,000
Waived fees	
Water and Sewer connection	$ 20,000
Building permit fee waiver	$ 4,300
Total	$ 1,549,300

2009 Expansion

Facilities upgrade grants	
Governor's Opportunity Fund - VEDP	$ 50,000
Tobacco Region Opportunity Fund Grant	$ 100,000
Virginia Jobs Investment Program Grant	$ 17,500
Enterprise Zone Jobs Grant	$ 80,000
Dept of Housing and Community Development Block Grant	$ 150,000
Local Contribution for Community Development Block Grant	$ 50,000
Waived fees	
Building permit fee waiver	$ 5,000
Total	$ 452,500

2017 Expansion

Facilities expansion grants	
Governor's Opportunity Fund - VEDP	$ 150,000
Tobacco Region Opportunity Fund Grant	$ 235,000
Tobacco Region Opportunity Fund Loan	$ 117,500
Total	$ 502,500
Grand Total	**$ 2,504,300**

10 GOVERNMENT SUBSIDIES FOR ORAN SAFETY GLASS[112]

Oran was supposed to provide jobs with solid pay in exchange for its subsidies, but there is evidence that it may not be meeting its performance benchmarks. One former employee complained in June of 2018 that:

> *I wouldn't recommend anyone to work at OSG because there is no job security...The life span seemed to be a year at the most. People there work for basically nothing and have families to feed. Some are hired through the temp agency and are only paid $8 per hour, but OSG may pay the temp service $10 per hour for that employee.[113]*

Late in 2014 the U.S. Equal Employment Opportunity Commission sued OSG under Title VII of the Civil Rights Act of 1964 for firing an assistant quality control supervisor, Nicole Williams. Williams began working at OSG on May 9, 2012. Around May 25, she learned she was pregnant, and notified the company a few days later. Although she was performing at an acceptable level, on June 8, OSG fired her because she was pregnant.

OSG was contractually obligated to create at least fifty new jobs in exchange for the subsidies it received to locate in Greensville in 2006. In 2008 it promised to create an additional 25 new jobs with an average annual wage of $33,648. OSG's performance agreement was careful to specify that "seasonal and temporary positions...shall not qualify as new jobs." In 2017, OSG's performance agreement was even more insistent about what qualified as meeting the contractual requirement for new jobs. It read:

> *New jobs mean a minimum of fifty-five (55) new full-time employees maintained at the existing facility and the New Facility for which the standard fringe benefits are provided by the Company for each employee, and for which the Company pays an average annual wage of at least $43,000.*

Those parameters don't jibe with word inside the factory about the heavy use of temporary workers. Although Greensville County has the right to demand proof of full time employment and wages at the factory,

---

[112] Virginia Freedom of Information Act release from the Virginia Economic Development Project. See https://IsraelLobby.org/Oran for details.

[113] Quote, with spelling corrections, from employer review website Indeed.com consulted on October 7, 2019.

and has been asked to release such information, it has provided no evidence that requirements in the performance agreement are being met.[114]

Other outstanding questions are whether VIAB is trading opportunities to lobbyists like Matthew Benka who are retained by projects such as Oran, for unpaid, and unreported "favors." Benka stewarded the VIAB reconstitution through the legislature, but never reported his lobbying work for VIAB or the Jewish federations pushing the reconstitution.

The greatest issue of concern to Virginians and Americans in general is that more military conflict in the Middle East will be good for Oran Safety Glass. Less conflict will be bad. Military contracts have been in eclipse, the likely result of Pentagon mistrust of Oran's contracting practices as well as declining numbers of American "boots on the ground" in the Middle East. This creates subtle pressure on VIAB, and the Virginia Jewish federation citizen lobbyists, and wider Israel affinity ecosystem who support OSG, to do something. What could be better than for the U.S. to follow Israel into a new round of on-the-ground military action against Israel's enemies, or be convinced to launch wars that benefit Israel on its own account? What could be better?

---

[114] The county indicated in response to a Virginia Freedom Of Information Act request for this data saying that "no such documents exist" about machinery, improvement and equipment costs and expenses at the Oran plant. The indicated that only Virginia's Commissioner of Revenue would have such information, and that it would be confidential. Greenfield County also does not know how many new jobs were created or maintained, and that "Job verification is managed by the grant agencies, on the county." See https://IsraelLobby.org/Oran for details.

7.
ISRAELI SETTLER IDENTITY LAUNDERING THROUGH PROJECT TURBINE

...we have a company that is building/spending... $100 million in real estate development this year. They're building solar energy farms in four different counties;... the alternative energy company is the major Israeli real estate firm...they are building in four counties right now and then roll into probably at least four more in the next 18 months; they're building their US office in Richmond—that's huge that's never happened before.[115] **Dov Hoch, VIAB Executive Director**

Handling 70 percent of world internet traffic takes acres of servers and mountains of telecommunications equipment. "Data Center Alley" in Northern Virginia houses the largest single concentration of data centers in the world. A result of spiraling demand for internet web services, data centers housing server and telecom infrastructure are not just one of Virginia's biggest energy consumers, data centers are one of the world's largest sources of global electricity demand. [116]

Major data centers, such as Amazon Web Services, say they want to power them with 100 percent renewable energy. Through the end of 2018, Amazon had invested in 53 renewable energy projects to deliver over a thousand megawatts of power. Six of Amazon's power investments are in Virginia and the company claimed its energy use was 50 percent renewable by year end 2018.[117]

---

[115] Hoc, Dov "What VIAB Does and How it Benefits Virginia" Speech at the Weinstein Jewish Community Center, April 4, 2019

[116] Clicking Clean Virginia: The Dirty Energy Powering Data Center Alley, Greenpeace, February 13, 2019,
https://www.greenpeace.org/usa/reports/click-clean-virginia/

[117] Froese, Michelle, "Amazon responds to Greenpeace report — remains committed to 100% renewables," Windpower Engineering Development, February 13, 2019, https://www.windpowerengineering.com/business-news-projects/amazon-responds-to-greenpeace-report-remains-committed-to-100-renewables/

Although data center users like Amazon claim they advocate for regulatory and tax policies at state and federal levels to promote renewable energy usage, at present the corporate commitment is entirely voluntary. On the supply side, electricity providers are sticking with the cheapest energy production options. Virginia's dominant power supplier, Dominion Energy, has only 4 percent of its generation mix coming from renewables with the rest derived from carbon-based fuels. The company's current goal increases renewables only to 10 percent by 2030. [118]

The Virginia Israel Advisory Board has a solution to data center energy needs: solar energy farms sold, designed, installed and administered by Israeli companies:

> *Project Turbine – A multi-billion dollar Israeli real estate and renewable energy concern with significant properties in D.C. and Northern Virginia is developing several solar energy sites in Virginia to produce electricity. Expanding renewable energy capacity is a requirement of major data centers to locate in Virginia.* **Virginia Israel Advisory Board 2018 Annual Report**

The offer sounds compelling. Data centers continue to buy energy from Dominion Energy and other power companies generated by fracked natural gas and other carbon based sources. VIAB is working behind the scenes to win business for Israel using VIAB's status as a government agency while hiding the true parent organization behind "Project Turbine." One prime example is the Mineral Gap Datacenter.

Mineral Gap Datacenter

VIAB Southwest Region Coordinator and Board Member Aviva Frye is a "caterer, licensed travel agent and community organizer of over 30 years." Holding a BA in Political Science from the University of Maryland and master's in International Relations from Boston University, her profile on VIAB's website says that, "with most of her family living in Israel, and Aviva in SW Virginia, she is thrilled to bring the two parts of her life together." Left off her VIAB bio is that she is the chairperson of "Rural VA Dems," a group with leaders drawn from the Central Committee of the Democratic Party of Virginia aiming to get Southwest Virginia non-

---

[118] "Integrated Resource Plan," Dominion Energy, 2018, p.173
https://www.dominionenergy.com/library/domcom/media/about-us/making-energy/2018-irp.pdf

urban dwellers to vote the party ticket.[119] At first, she would not seem to be the ideal candidate to sell complex Israeli solar energy solutions in Virginia. But her role was not sales, it was market entry. So, in addition to roles at VIAB and the state Democratic Party, Frye is also the Director of Regulation and Public Relations for Caden-Energix.

Energix is a small renewable energy producer founded in 2009 and traded on the Israeli stock exchange. Alony Hetz—a private company—has been the controlling shareholder of Energix ever since it was founded.

Energix Renewable Energy Ltd is deeply invested in territories illegally occupied by Israel in the Palestinian West Bank. Energix also owns a solar farm located in the Meitarim illegal settlement industrial zone in the Israeli occupied Syrian Golan Heights.[120] Energix allegedly used "questionable methods" to obtain access to land from its indigenous Syrian-Druze owners. The Druze stood in the way of Energix developing a wind energy project.

Alony Hetz also has investments in illegal settlements. It invested in the illegal settlement of Ariel in the occupied Palestinian West Bank. It holds a 58.22 percent stake in an Israeli real estate firm that owns Amot Ariel in the Ariel West Industrial Zone.[121] Other Alony-Hetz investments in the United States include Carr Properties, a U.S.-based real estate investment trust (or REIT) that owns properties in the Washington D.C. area and Boston (a 43.65 percent stake). Alony Hetz proudly owns and trumpets on its website a 114,000 square foot "trophy" property in Old Town, Alexandria.

Caden Energy was the brainchild of former CEO of Century Media Records CEO Robert Caden. In 2015 CMR was acquired by Sony Music Entertainment, and Caden went looking to start up other ventures. In 2018 Energix and Alony Hetz acquired a 58 percent stake in a series of Caden Energy solar projects in Arizona and Virginia for $13 million, "with a total capacity of hundreds of megawatts." Energix does not manufacture equipment. The four Virginia sites initially announced acquisition of panels from First Solar, an American solar panel manufacturer and a seller of utility-scale power plants. Energix also has not traditionally had its own construction teams. Rather, it hires contractors to build out the sites, after receiving the proper permits. Energix is interested in high-margin project sales, contracting, and administration of solar arrays, including selling

---

[119] Rural Caucus of the Democratic Party of Virginia, Rural VA Dems, consulted October 3, 2019, https://www.ruralvadems.org/

[120] "Energix Group" Who Profits – The Israeli Occupation Industry.
https://whoprofits.org/company/energix-group-0/

[121] "Alony-Hetz Properties & Investments LTD," American Friends Service Committee, updated June 25, 2019
https://investigate.afsc.org/company/alony-hetz

excess electricity to local utilities. One critical phase for any solar project is permitting. Aviva Frye's job was getting state approval for those permits. But when Frye approached government officials, she did so in her capacity as a board member of VIAB.

In February 2018 Frye set up a meeting and demanded follow-up from Angela Navarro, Deputy Secretary of Natural Resources at the Office of the Governor. Caden-Energix wanted Navarro to know that a Kentucky Utilities Company and its subsidiary, Old Dominion Power Company, ODP, was not going to provision solar energy for the Mineral Gap Data Center. ODP serves 30,000 customers in Western Virginia. According to an email about Frye's efforts obtained through the Virginia Freedom of Information Act, Frye said:

> *Kentucky Utilities has made it clear to Energix that they are uninterested in providing renewable energy in Wise. The data center, which is already there, wants to expand. Del Kilgore [Delegate Terry Kilgore, Virginia House of Delegates] told us that at least two other data centers want to locate in Wise County if the renewable energy were available. But they MUST have solar power, hence the utility company is keeping good jobs out of Wise County.[122]*

The data center "which is already there" is the aforementioned Mineral Gap, a high-security 65,000 square foot data colocation center on a 22-acre site in Wise County. The facility was backed by $350,000 in Tobacco Region Opportunity Funds. Whether there is enough market demand for capacity at the data center in the isolated, rural western part of Virginia is not yet clear. Server space is currently being sold as an extra secure facility owing to its sheer physical remoteness.

When Frye met with government officials across the state to steer contracts and funding toward the Israeli solar energy company she represents, she did it on the basis of her role at VIAB. Two weeks after Governor Ralph Northam was sworn in as Virginia's newly elected governor on January 13, 2018, Frye sought a private meeting with First Lady Pamela Northam. The meeting was to talk about Energix, but Frye signed the request for the meeting as the "Southwest Coordinator of the Virginia Israel Advisory Board."

---

[122] "The Virginia-Israel Advisory Board Taxpayer-Funded Israel Lobbying Inside State Government - Reconstitution from Governor's Office to the Legislature " IRmep, The Israel Lobby Archive, https://IsraelLobby.org/viab/

Cary, David (GOV)

From:	Aviva Frye <aviva@viab.org>
Sent:	Friday, January 26, 2018 8:24 AM
To:	Cary, David (GOV)
Subject:	Appointment with First Lady

Dear David:

I hope this email finds you doing well .
I would like to set an appointment to meet with the First Lady, if possible some time next week, to discuss some projects through the Governor's Virginia Israel Advisory Board as well as the investments in Virginia by Energix, the Israeli renewable energy company, I run in the United States.
I can be reached at 276-451-4428.

Thank you for your attention,

Aviva S. Frye
Virginia Israel Advisory Bd
SouthWest Coordinator

Sent from my iPhone

11 AVIVA FRYE MEETING REQUEST ON BEHALF OF ENERGIX AS A VIAB OFFICIAL

Caden Energix applied for its permits and is now moving fast in rural and northern Virginia to build systems. Caden Energix's first rural solar project to go public with an announced location and status update is located in Gladys, Virginia in the state's southwest. As Senior Vice President Ken Niemann explained, "The site in Gladys also has an existing Dominion Energy transmission line that we will tie into, thus eliminating the need to construct new electric lines off-site." Caden Energix practices are not always environmentally friendly. In order to find sites in less densely populated areas that don't require paying prime farmland prices, some property acquisition necessitates clearcutting stands of timber in order to launch projects.[123]

A permit application to build out the 1,108 acre Gladys site says it will produce 60 megawatts, that is, after the trees have been clear cut, the equipment is installed, and it gets connected to the transmission system.[124]

Real estate expertise is vital since Caden Energix leases land for up to 35 years. It then says it will remove its equipment and return the land to the owner or heirs. Solar panel manufacturer warrantees usually don't

---

[123] Phillips, Jenn, "Solar farm meeting held in Gladys," The Altavista Journal, July 19, 2019. http://www.altavistajournal.com/news/article_a5dc1f6c-aa16-11e9-9280-670d9aa0c511.html

[124]"General Notice - Caden Energix Gladys LLC -Notice of Intent - Small Renewable Energy Project (Solar)," Virginia Regulatory Town Hall, consulted 10/3/2019
https://www.townhall.virginia.gov/L/ViewNotice.cfm?gnid=1021

guarantee power generation above 20 percent of original capacity beyond 20 years as the efficiency of the panels degrades.

In a 2018 periodic update, Energix admitted in a footnote that it did not expect to be able to sell solar energy in Virginia at above-market rates.[125] It remains to be seen whether VIAB and other solar energy advocates in Virginia can change state law so that energy from their solar farms must by law be purchased by Dominion Energy or other utilities operating in Virginia at higher rates. If that can be done, an already installed base of solar arrays will produce much higher returns for their beneficial owners.

The locations of three other sites with pending permits that have not been publicly announced indicate that another offtake strategy Energix may be depending on is VIAB's portfolio of other projects. One site, near Wythe, Virginia for 20 megawatts just happens to be located next to a large energy consumer—a PepsiCo bottling plant.[126] Could Energix work down through the Sabra-PepsiCo joint venture to sign an offtake agreement with the plant? Another Energix permit application site for 82.5 megawatts happens to be located just 11.4 miles from the Oran Safety Glass plant north of Emporia. [127]

There is perhaps no image more symbolic of VIAB benefitting from state funding than its office in the 5,500-square-foot Southwest Virginia Energy Center located in Bristol, Virginia. It was built with $8 million in Tobacco Commission funds at a construction cost of $5 million. It is supposed to house research, manufacturing and "clean fuel energy products and systems" developers. But it has a single non-government tenant, a lone iPhone app developer.

The only other tenant is VIAB Southwest Region Coordinator Aviva Frye, using the facility as a comfortable perch to advance VIAB and her Caden-Energix projects in what she told the news media is the state sanctioned mission to bring "businesses from Israel to Virginia."[128]

---

[125] Energix – Renewal Energies Ltd., Periodic Report for 2018,
http://www.energix-group.com/uploads/1558340078.pdf

[126] "General Notice - Caden Energix Wytheville LLC-Notice of Intent - Small Renewable Energy Project (Solar)," Virginia Regulatory Town Hall, consulted 10/3/2019
https://www.townhall.virginia.gov/L/ViewNotice.cfm?gnid=1024

[127] "General Notice - Caden Energix Jarratt LLC-Notice of Intent - Small Renewable Energy Project (Solar)," Virginia Regulatory Town Hall, consulted 10/3/2019
https://www.townhall.virginia.gov/L/ViewNotice.cfm?gnid=1023

[128] McGee, David, "Energy center finally has tenants, but facility still mostly vacant" Herald Courier, April 20, 2016
https://www.heraldcourier.com/news/energy-center-finally-has-tenants-but-

But the four overt Caden-Energix projects overseen from Frye's isolated southern outpost are not the full extent of Alony Hetz Energix solar development activities in Virginia. Across northern Virginia, it appears that "Project Turbine" is quietly working behind three opaque shell companies to sign as many 30-year leases with Virginia public schools and other entities as it possibly can. A small portion of the electricity from the installations is sold at a discount to the school system, while the front companies sell the excess production back to the local electric utility grid. As a bonus, schools can use off-the-shelf curriculum for students to learn about renewable energy, allegedly making the solar arrays an educational benefit to the school.

IDENTITY LAUNDERING THROUGH SUN TRIBE

Energix and Alony Hetz solar farming efforts for the Mineral Gap Datacenter are moving forward, but not under the Caden-Energix brand. On paper, Aviva Frye appears no longer to have any connection to the project, since activities have shifted to technical proposals and land acquisition. But there are four clues that Energix and Alony Hetz are still involved.

The first is that in its July 18, 2017 board meeting, Aviva Frye explained that "Energix's visit to Virginia resulted in an MOU [memorandum of understanding] in Wise to put up a solar field for a beta company."[129]

Energix and Alony Hetz are operating as the beneficial owner of a "beta company" shell entity. The name of the company now developing Mineral Gap data center in Wise County is Sun Tribe Solar LLC. At Mineral Gap, Sun Tribe Solar will benefit not only from Virginia State funding flowing into the project, but also $500,000 from the U.S. Department of Treasury paid as part of a $10 million grant for solar energy development on abandoned mine lands.[130]

---

facility-still-mostly-vacant/article_ec457b5c-b2a8-53b9-9925-0a8467d11153.html

[129] Virginia Israel Advisory Board, meeting minutes, July 18, 2017, https://vchr.org/viab_foia_responses/07182017.html

[130] "Wise County: $500,000 for development of a solar energy system for the Mineral Gap Data Center." Times News, July 31, 2019 https://www.timesnews.net/Government/2019/07/31/Data-center-gets-500-000-federal-grant-for-solar-power-system

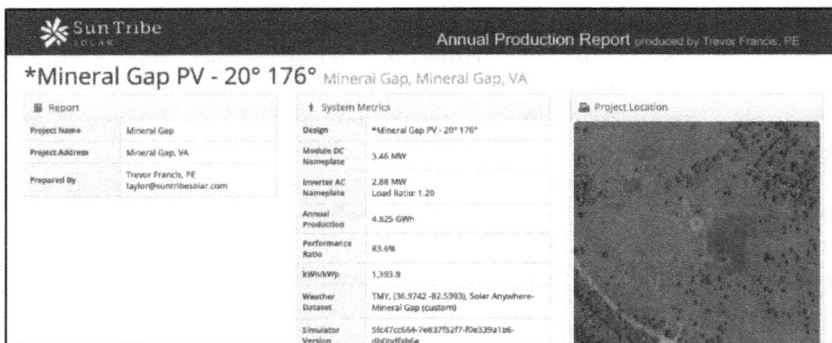

12 SUN TRIBE SOLAR MINERAL GAP PROPOSAL

The second tipoff that Alony Hetz and Energix are behind the Sun Tribe Solar front-companies developing Virginia solar projects was the July 1, 2019 announcement that Bill Nusbaum was joining the VIAB board as a nominee of the General Assembly of Virginia.[131] Nusbaum is a partner doing "economic development" for Williams Mullen, a regionally based law firm with 240 attorneys in Virginia, Washington DC, North Carolina and South Carolina. In 2014, VIAB was working on entering into a partnership with a law firm to sell to government and overcome regulatory issues, noting in meeting minutes that:

> *VIAB has created a program where a Virginia boutique law firm will work with the VIAB to identify Israeli companies with high tech products and/or development capabilities that can team with Virginia companies that fall in the "special set aside categories." It is expected that the companies can identify opportunities within the government segment. This can offer unique opportunities for Israeli companies to navigate the complicated US government contracting bureaucracy while offering Virginia companies to expand their offerings. It is expected that future manufacturing and/or assembly requirements will take place in Virginia and that the VIAB will guide the job creating expansion that will result from the program.[132]*

So where is the connection? The law firm of Williams Mullen has intimate ties to Sun Tribe Solar. In February of 2016, Williams Mullen

---

[131] "Bill Nusbaum Named to Virginia Israel Advisory Board" Williams Mullen, July 1, 2019 https://www.williamsmullen.com/news/bill-nusbaum-named-virginia-israel-advisory-board

[132] Virginia Israel Advisory Board, meeting minutes, July 29, 2014

Partner Philip Goodpasture filed articles of organization for a new limited liability company called Sun Tribe Solar with the Virginia Division of Corporations. The filing was followed by two more, one in 2016 for Sun Tribe Holdings by Williams Mullins Senior Associate Richard Palmieri, and yet another for Sun Tribe Development LLC by Taylor Brown with Goodpasture as his agent. Taylor Brown is listed as co-founder of Sun Tribe Solar.

13 SUN TRIBE SOLAR, LLC BUSINESS ENTITY DETAILS[133]

Many of Sun Tribe's direct competitors, such as the case of Arlington County Public Schools bidding discussed later, are transparent public corporations in which the source of capital, financial wherewithal and beneficial owners are publicly known. Not true for Sun Tribe, which strives to hide its true ownership. It is probable that Philip Goodpasture is not a newly minted solar energy entrepreneur, but rather the nominee of anonymous beneficial owners, whose identities are hidden and excluded from all of Sun Tribe's contracts and disclosures made to win business. In legalese, Williams Mullen is serving as the "formation agent" and service provider that will do ongoing legal maintenance of the company entities. In this particular case, the primary reason Sun Tribe would be set up via three separate LLCs is so that it can be owned and managed anonymously. Energix and Alony Hetz can then use the Virginia based LLCs to fund via international wire transfer the seed capital Sun Tribe needs to market, sell

---

[133] Virginia State Division of Corporations database.

and set up solar energy projects that return its investment over 25 to 30 to 35 years. Williams Mullen will then transfer net income back to Energix and Alony Hetz. If the operation gets into trouble, the nominee can transfer the ownership of operation to intermediary offshore shell companies, sell Sun Tribe, cash out through an initial public offering on a U.S. stock exchange or even claim bankruptcy and roll it up without ever publicly implicating the true beneficial owners.

While Caden-Energix might have been able to operate more or less openly in more remote projects in Southern Virginia without too much risk of exposure or pushback, in the north of the state and academic markets everywhere, the risk that Alony Hetz could be exposed in the sensitive markets it targets requires anonymity. Creating a pleasant corporate image is therefore key.

Sun Tribe's business development operation is already a social media and marketing powerhouse. Though it only joined Twitter in May of 2019, the @SunTribeSolar feed is full of hip postings. Sun Tribe's young workers enjoy biking to work. They are recent graduates of Virginia universities. Their dogs are welcome in the office. One canine is even pictured sitting at the conference table giving input. Young engineers are encouraged to apply to work for Sun Tribe, and many of their profiles appear in the feed.

Sun Tribe Solar @SunTribeSolar · Aug 14

We're a dog-friendly #solar office, but sometimes they insist on managing our meetings. Here's Duncan running the show in a @VaultVirginia conference room (photo: @cramerphoto). Want to join us? Click below. #dogsoftwitter

suntribesolar.com/careers/

14 SUN TRIBE SOLAR TWEET ABOUT DOGS ON AUGUST 14, 2019

90

In a July 15 post, Chief Strategy Officer David Welch stresses Sun Tribe's local roots. "As a Virginia-based company, we're proud of the fact that the commonwealth is embracing a 21st-century economy built on the foundation of clean, affordable energy."

One of Sun Tribe's key strategies is obtaining nearly zero cost long-term leases on land in exchange for giving landowners a small discount on electricity generated by their solar arrays. Sun Tribe sometimes wins projects through no-bid contracts directly with school superintendents. Other installations are a result of school board proposal requests to multiple firms. The vetting and contracting process never broaches the issue of Sun Tribe's beneficial owners, though some public stakeholders are beginning to question the wisdom of contracting with thinly capitalized LLCs.

ARE ALONY HETZ AND ENERGIX NOW OCCUPYING VIRGINIA PUBLIC SCHOOL SYSTEM ROOFTOPS?

In Virginia's King William Public Schools system, superintendent David White was informed about Sun Tribe from Middlesex County Public Schools Superintendent Peter Gretz.[467] Gretz had executed a contract with Sun Tribe on November 7, 2017 to "construct, own operate and maintain a solar array on school property, at no cost to the school system." Gretz sold the idea to the Board of Supervisors on the basis that,

> *Power will be purchased from Sun Tribe Solar at a rate of 6.8 cents per KW from Sun Tribe, versus the 9.5 cents per KW that they pay currently.*[135]

Gretz's decision enjoyed fawning media coverage. *The Washington Post* hailed it with the headline, "Virginia schools have seen the light, and it's

---

[134] Luck, Ashley, "Three King William schools to be powered by solar panel project," Daily Press, February 12, 2019
https://www.dailypress.com/virginiagazette/va-vg-tr-kw-suntribe-solar-project-20190125-story.html

[135] Middlesex County Board of Supervisors, Meeting Minutes, December 5, 2017, page 3
https://www.co.middlesex.va.us/Board%20of%20Supervisors/BOS%20Pac kets/2017/12-5-17%20Packet.pdf

solar," quoting Gretz, "All of us are telling the same story, all trying to deal with budgetary challenges…. this is just such a no-brainer."[136]

White's board then too "reached out to Sun Tribe" to start discussing an agreement for "three of our schools." In February 2019 King Williams County Public Schools signed a 30 year agreement with Sun Tribe under which it will allow the company to install 4,500 solar panels on adjacent land. Sun Tribe will sell electricity to schools at a small discount compared to standard Dominion Energy power rates, while under some contracts selling excess production to utilities and other buyers.

In late 2018 Arlington Public Schools also contracted with Sun Tribe Solar to install 6,980 panels under a 25-year contract. Arlington School Board chair Reid Goldstein said the Sun Tribe award was the result of a 2017 strategic plan. The school system issued a request for proposals and received six responses. It rejected one for failing to provide mandatory information, and another for not meeting "joint venture" status. Of the remaining three, Ameresco, WGL Energy Systems, and Sun Tribe, Sun Tribe won out.[46:]

But how far behind Sun Tribe's corporate veil did these school boards and superintendents probe to discover its origins, source of capital, ability to deliver on multi-decade contracts and expertise? Not at all. In public meetings during the Sun Tribe proposal review process and final contracts, Alony Hetz and Energix ties to unlawful activities in occupied territories also never came up.

Other project stakeholders, such as students, parents and local taxpayers might not want their school doing business with opaque fronts for an Israeli company that profits directly from illegal Israeli settlements. Alony Hetz, Energix and VIAB's obvious response, if the true owners ever emerge from behind their corporate veil, would be predictable. "Don't you want to avert the climate change crisis by harnessing solar energy? Are you against new economy jobs for young people (who own cute dogs?)"

With no shortage of U.S. solar start-ups as well as experienced, completely transparent Virginia vendors, stakeholders' response might be simple. "Yes, we want solar, yes, we want jobs. We just don't want an Israeli occupation of our rooftops and territories until Palestinians regain their human rights. Especially not at public schools. It just sets the wrong example."

---

[136] Truong, Debbie, "Virginia Schools have seen the light, and it's solar," The Washington Post, March 24, 2019.

[137] Request for Conceptual Proposals 01FY18, Solar Photovoltaic Rooftop System Installation and Sale of Generated Electricity, Arlington Public Schools, public hearing, July 13, 2018, https://www.apsva.us/wp-content/uploads/2018/07/RFP-01FY18-Solar-Power-PPT.pdf

Energix and Alony Hetz are clearly in an all-out race to build as many solar arrays as quickly as possible, while VIAB and other industry groups work on Virginia regulators. The most profitable scenario would be a new state law mandating small scale solar energy production be purchased at higher prices by utilities through net metering in recognition of the higher cost to produce solar energy.

However, in the meantime, Governor Northam has signed into law and issued executive orders mandating 3,000 megawatts of solar and wind power energy must be in production by year 2028. Dominion Energy must procure electricity from smaller scale solar energy producers in the amount of 50 megawatts in 2019, buying 150 by year 2022. Utilities such as Appalachian Power must meet 25 percent of the new targets by signing Power-Purchase Agreements with smaller scale projects.[138] The governor is clearly doing his part for VIAB and the solar industry.

For VIAB, a looming government-mandated "offtake agreement" is even better than Project Jonah's proposed arrangement, explored in the next chapter, to sell tilapia to a regional supermarket chain. It could even prevail against popular opposition to beneficial owners of that solar power, that is, if the public is ever allowed to find out.

DO SUN TRIBE SOLUTIONS SERVE PUBLIC SCHOOLS?

Assuming public school administrators don't know about the hidden costs of supporting illegal settlements, does contracting with Sun Tribe Solar still make sense? The relevant costs for solar energy farms are the purchase price, installation costs, and the cost of land. In a Sun Tribe deal, the costs normally covered by the purchase price are more than covered by the customer giving away the land and agreeing to purchase energy from Sun Tribe. Does the purchaser ever truly understand or share in any of the potential gains?

A close inspection of Sun Tribe's contract[139] with Hamilton Holmes Middle School provides some answers. Under its "lease" agreement, Sun Tribe Solar will pay a dollar per year for the large tract of ground necessary for a 478 kilowatt direct current solar farm. It will have all the rights of

---

[138] "Expanding Access to Clean Energy and Growing the Clean Energy Jobs of the Future," Executive Order, Office of the Governor, Commonwealth of Virginia, Number 43, 2019
https://www.governor.virginia.gov/media/governorvirginiagov/executive-actions/EO-43-Expanding-Access-to-Clean-Energy-and-Growing-the-Clean-Energy-Jobs-of-the-Future.pdf
[139] Obtained via VFOIA from the school system.

owning the site for three decades, but few of the obligations. For example, Sun Tribe will issue a set of security requirements that the school must follow to protect the site against intrusion, vandalism, or other problems. The school will suffer some environmental degradation to get solar energy. In order to prepare the site, a large stand of trees will have to be clear cut by Sun Tribe Solar.

Hamilton Holmes, in addition to giving away land usage, is also giving away the upside potential, given its intended use. According to the signed facility contract, Sun Tribe will be generating four times as much energy as the school needs. The excess will be sold at commercial rates to Dominion, which it is obligated to purchase under current law. Although most of the contract documents portray the agreement as a "negotiation," the school system did not bring in any independent consultant to evaluate the terms to negotiate a share of "net metering" revenue sales to Dominion. Although it was offered the possibility to undertake more risk in exchange for a small piece of the upside, the sale was geared toward getting the school to buy power at a slightly reduced rate with no equity or profit sharing. A savvy school that examined all the numbers might have come up with better terms, such as entirely free solar electricity as a condition for the land lease to host a solar array. But neither Arlington nor King William County public school system boards evaluating Sun Tribe Solar proposals appeared to bring in independent expert advisors before signing a contract.

So, under its signed contract, not only is Hamilton Holmes not getting free electricity, it is obligated to pay Sun Tribe for electricity. If the Sun Tribe system had been installed and running in 2018, referencing the school's actual utility bill energy consumption and Sun Tribe's contractual requirements, the school would have paid Sun Tribe $51,000 for electricity that year, vs what it actually paid Dominion which was $58,000. However, Sun Tribe over the same year would have made $178,000 selling the excess power to Dominion.

It might be argued that Sun Tribe's installation and operation of the site combined with the small discount on energy is enough to make it a good deal for the Hamilton Holmes. Not true.

The industry average installed cost for such facilities is only $1.03 per watt, or around half a million dollars to build the entire Hamilton solar farm. If Hamilton were to cancel the deal after a year, its contract requires the school pay $1.2 million to Sun Tribe, which would stand to gain a tidy $700,000 profit after installation cost. But what about operation and maintenance? The costs after installation are minimal for solar electricity, and the school has already agreed to absorb costs to provide security against theft or vandalism at the site.

There are also economic externalities associated with such solar installations. In economics, a negative externality is a cost that is suffered by a third party as a consequence of an economic transaction. In this transaction, the "generator" (Sun Tribe) and the "customer" (Hamilton Holmes Middle School) are the first and second parties, and Dominion Energy is the third party whose resources are indirectly and negatively affected. The intermittent nature of solar is a major issue.

Under the contract—and in reality—Dominion Energy is expected to provide 100 percent of the electricity demand of the school no matter what is happening at the solar array. For solar, this means whenever it is dark, or the system is out of commission for any number of reasons. A true "off the grid" solar system would charge costly arrays of batteries to power the customer through such periods. At Hamilton School, Sun Tribe's battery is Dominion Energy. This externality creates environmental consequences that remove some of the ecological luster from solar.

Dominion Energy's gas, nuclear and other plants have to cover 100 percent of the school's needs, whether it requires power or not. In a study one regional utility, Duke Energy, claims that since nuclear plants can't ramp up and down to mitigate the intermittency of solar, it ramps up carbon-based production to cover such peaks. It further claims that extensive use of solar in its North Carolina market is increasing carbon emissions.[140]

Sun Tribe has other rights under its sales agreements, including reassignment to another company. It is free to sell the site to another company, go public and sell shares to the public while retaining majority ownership, and boost real returns in other ways. The school, on the other hand, is obligated to convince any assignee to continue buying power from the system. Like Virginia Tech's memorandum of understanding with Sabra Dipping Company, it is reduced to the role of performing sales and market maintenance for Sun Tribe as a junior partner.

Sun Tribe and Caden-Energix and Alony Hetz are scouring Virginia for grants and subsidies for solar on the premise that they produce jobs and tax revenues. Neither is true. They only boost potential insider profits. While in the case of Hamilton Holmes Public School, the solar farm will entail some construction jobs, they will only be temporary. Full time equivalent jobs (FTE) required to administer the farm are close to zero. As verified in Sun Tribe's own proposals, there is also no tax consequence

---

[140] Van der Vaart, Donald, "North Carolina Energy Company Finds Solar Power Actually Increases Pollution," The Federalist, October 4, 2019 https://thefederalist.com/2019/10/04/north-carolina-energy-company-finds-solar-power-actually-increases-pollution/

for the project. Other than the temporary construction jobs, it will contribute no net revenue to the local, county or state treasury.

The school gets little for the land give away. While boasting rights for having a solar farm are clearly worth something, the net financial benefit is paltry. An independent model using actual 2018 electricity costs and Sun Tribe contractual discounts yields a net present value over 25 years of electricity savings to Hamilton Holmes of only around $134,000.

What about for the true beneficial owners of Sun Tribe in Israel and elsewhere? One thing that is notable about the Hamilton contract is that near the end of negotiations Sun Tribe suddenly wrote into its contracts an option to administer the site for an additional five years for a total of 30 years. That may be due to not only a drastic ongoing decline in the price of solar panels, but an increase in their productive life span.[141] Solar panels are now producing at high rates much longer than has previously been the case.

So, what is in it for Sun Tribe's beneficial owners is a 600 percent return on investment. Let's again go to our hypothetical case of the Hamilton Holmes system being installed in 2018 and run for 25 years. At expected current rates of solar panel efficiency, and forecast inflation, Sun Tribe would produce a net present value[142] of $3 million in excess "net metered" sales to Dominion Energy. Or to put it another way, the Israeli owner and VIAB insiders and investors have the potential to skim six times as much "cream" from the project as the "milk" (construction jobs and tax revenue) touted to ordinary Virginians. They are producing all of the high-end value added to the project in terms of public relations, design, legal work securing permitting and management of leases, insurance and contracts. There may be even future investment banking work involved to take Sun Tribe public on a U.S. stock exchange to cash out. However, only low value-added jobs are available to the junior partners in construction, monitoring and maintenance.

The Hamilton Holmes project faced grassroots political pushback in 2019. On September 30, King William County Public Schools superintendent David White contacted project manager Alex Gregory at Sun Tribe Solar:

---

[141] "Solar Electricity Costs" citing the National Renewable Energy Laboratory, and expert studies at http://www.solarcellcentral.com/cost_page.html

[142] Net Present Value is the current day "lump sum" value of money expected from future cash inflows and outflows. Like an "offtake" agreement, a solid NPV calculation backed by a contract can allow a company to access capital from investors and calculate its own profits. A high NPV from a portfolio of contracts increases a company's value for the purposes of its own sale or initial public offering.

> *Alex, we have a local T.E.A. Party that is extremely active as it is an election year. That being the case, would Sun Tribe provide some answers or talking points to questions they are asking on their website?[143]*

Sun Tribe immediately offered help to quell the unrest. But Sun Tribe's public relations challenge wasn't with the "local T.E.A." party, but 22 miles to the northeast in Tappahannock, VA. There, a group called the Essex County Conservation Alliance was publicizing a fully sourced 18 page study compiling concerns about solar energy farms in the Tidewater counties of Virginia.[144] The T.E.A. party had only posted it on their website.

Rob Corradi, Public Affairs and Development Manager at Sun Tribe forwarded White's concerns to his team, saying:

> *"I'm happy to write up some stuff for them to use/have in their back pocket for knowledge. But for broader visibility (and considering some of what they're saying here impacts the UDev (University market development) side as well—looping in Devin [Welch, Chief Strategy and Development Officer], Taylor [Brown, chief technical officer] , Seth [Herman, Senior Development Manager] and Danny [Van Clief, former Coronal Energy President, newly leading large-scale development business] for awareness."[145]*

Sun Tribe had a reason to be worried about the university market. Students would not likely take kindly to unanswered concerns about solar energy as Sun Tribe ruthlessly targeted the university market. But what were the Essex County Conservation Alliance's concerns?

Key concerns were that solar energy farms were taking farmland out of productive use and destroying wooded areas. They argued that the term solar energy "farm" had its origin in the fact that solar companies found it cost effective to lease farmland in rural counties on which to erect their

---

[143] Correspondence released under the Virginia Freedom of Information Act by the King William County Public Schools. See: King Williams County Schools superintendent David White forwards concerns expressed by local groups to Sun Tribe Solar. Http://IsraelLobby.org/Suntribe/09302019_email_R.pdf

[144] The Essex County Conservation Alliance. "Industrial Solar Farms: An In-Depth Look at How Industrial Solar Farms Impact the Rural Tidewater Counties of the Middle Peninsula and Northern Neck."

[145] Correspondence released under the Virginia Freedom of Information Act by the King William County Public Schools. See: King Williams County Schools superintendent David White forwards concerns expressed by local groups to Sun Tribe Solar. Http://IsraelLobby.org/Suntribe/09302019_email_R.pdf

solar generation panels because land cleared for farming is already exposed to direct sunlight.

But the Essex County Conservation Alliance believes solar "farms" is a misnomer. They believe that in all cases such sites should undergo a rezoning process to become industrial use areas because a solar farm is an industrial enterprise that is wholly unrelated to and not supportive of any farm or forestry use. The construction of a solar power generation site on land previously dedicated to farming in reality undermines the underlying farm utility because the site is typically cleared of much of its topsoil, compacted and then chemically treated to control plant growth.

Worse, the costly recycling of solar panels, which contain many toxic chemicals, are costs not built typically into the business model. The Essex County Conservation Alliance feared those future costs might fall into the lap of the county. So, their final position is that an environmental impact survey and economic survey of solar farms driving down property values and tourism be conducted in conjunction with every solar "farm" project.

The Essex County Conservation Alliance's major concerns lead directly to the question of the economic vitality of limited liability solar energy companies like Sun Tribe Solar LLC. What happens when LLCs go bankrupt? They noted that solar farms can be shuttered and leave the county holding the bag:

> *"The solar farm corporation that leases the farmland is almost always a limited liability company, often thinly capitalized under a business model propped up by energy tax credits and legislative incentives. There is no guarantee that it will stay in business for the term of the lease, or, if it goes out of business, that it will have the financial resources to pay the waste clean-up and decommissioning costs. There are many solar farm LLCs that have declared bankruptcy in recent years."*[146]

In short, the Essex County Conservation Alliance's key question leads directly to the economic viability of Sun Tribe LLC. This, in turn, leads to the question of whether Energix or Alony Hetz could ever be compelled to clean up installations at the end of lengthy leases. But the Sun Tribe team couldn't, and didn't respond to these questions. After getting no response, Rob Corradi apparently decided to brief White with some talking points by phone, rather than writing, so there would be plausible deniability:

---

[146] The Essex County Conservation Alliance. "Industrial Solar Farms: An In-Depth Look at How Industrial Solar Farms Impact the Rural Tidewater Counties of the Middle Peninsula and Northern Neck."

I'll put together some facts/ talking points that you can sent [sic] to Dr. White, but I know I haven't reached out directly. Might be best if that continued contact comes from you.

I'd also say that we'd be happy to help him answer any specific questions that pop up in the future -- that he knows he can use us as a resource if he's getting inquiries he's not sure how to respond to from stakeholders.

And while I wouldn't put this part in writing, I'd maybe let him know that we've seen pockets of opposition to solar pop up in other communities throughout Virginia, and the opposition isn't grounded in any kind of real facts or genuine questions, but usually by people who are just looking for ways to object because they're anti-renewable energy on broad political grounds (which is likely what he's seeing here), have heard seen stuff on the internet that isn't true but people aren't particularly knowledgable [sic] about the science, or are generally a bit NIMBY-ish. [not in my backyard][147]

Perhaps as greater numbers of non-VIAB insiders understand the consequences to taxpayers and potentially to the environment of the predatory deals motivating Sun Tribe and Energix and Alony Hetz to contract as many solar systems to mostly unsuspecting, under advised, but land-holding public school officials as possible, the "pockets of opposition" will become more effective.

---

[147] Correspondence released under the Virginia Freedom of Information Act by the King William County Public Schools. See: King Williams County Schools superintendent David White forwards concerns expressed by local groups to Sun Tribe Solar. Http://IsraelLobby.org/Suntribe/09302019_email._R.pdf

8.

PROJECT JONAH TARGETS A SOCIALLY CONSCIOUS MARKET LEADER

All Board members are asked to refer to the project by this code name [Jonah]. Leaked information could jeopardize funding opportunities from the State. **VIAB Board Meeting Minutes**

Project Jonah has long been one of VIAB's biggest, most sacred projects. Secrecy has been considered to be paramount to success. One can almost imagine VIAB board members turning to cast furtive glances over their shoulders during a key 2013 meeting to see if any enemies or potential competitors were listening. According to minutes from that meeting, VIAB summed up the reason behind all the secrecy. "All Board members are asked to refer to the project by this code name. [Jonah] Leaked information could jeopardize funding opportunities from the State."[148]

In the bible, Jonah was running away from a God-given task in Nineveh by boat. God raised a mighty storm as a sign of his anger at Jonah. The vessel's sailors correctly surmised that Jonah was to blame for their peril, and tossed him overboard. Jonah was then swallowed by a "great fish," sent by God. Jonah began to pray to god for help and repent. After three days, God had the great fish vomit Jonah onto the shores of Nineveh to get back to the task at hand.

If VIAB were to rewrite Jonah as a three-act play, it would go a little something like this. A giant Israeli tilapia sees small tilapia fry eking out an existence in Virginia. Local aquatic creatures encourage him to cross the Atlantic to live with them. The Israeli tilapia obliges, arriving to swallow the local small fry and take over their pond.

The actual story of Project Jonah, while not a biblical tale, is deeply, morbidly fascinating. Local news media, if they had ever troubled themselves to ask questions and dig into the story a bit, could have discovered a great number of disturbing facts about "Project Jonah" and probably saved the state millions in unrecoverable losses in the bargain.

---

[148] VIAB Board Meeting Minutes, August 1, 2013.

The details are all readily available in regulatory filings, site permits, tax records and VIAB meeting minutes. Most important are the files of key funders such as the Tobacco Commission and Virginia Economic Development Partnership. But as the project soldiered on through the years, VIAB's leadership needed to have no fear, for no reporter from any major Virginia news media ever bothered looking deeply into Project Jonah. It may be a case of never looking a gift tilapia in the mouth.

Project Jonah is a fish farming project. VIAB, after identifying a proposed Israeli partner, began putting together the massive project. In a venture capital deal, an offtake agreement is a signed contract in which a purchaser agrees to buy quantities of a seller's product. It is negotiated in most instances even before the seller breaks ground on his production facility. The producer then uses the signed agreement to secure financing for construction, new equipment and startup costs. It is the present day proof of existing demand for future goods that gives venture capital investors the confidence to finance a project. But Project Jonah financiers so far appear to lack such confidence in VIAB.

VIAB WORKS ON AQUAMAOF'S "OFFTAKE AGREEMENT" AND VENTURE CAPITAL

On October 22, 2013 VIAB organized meetings between its Israeli fish farm partners and the Food City supermarket chain headquartered in Abingdon, just fifty miles to the south of the proposed fish farm plant site surrounding the Richlands wastewater treatment plant. The name of the Israeli partner, never mentioned in Virginia or mainstream U.S. press, is AquaMaof. "Aqua" is of course Latin for "water" and "Maof" is a Hebrew word meaning "flight" or "vision."

Food City was a logical partner for an offtake agreement with a major fish farm. Founded in 1955, the chain grew to 123 stores in Virginia, Kentucky, Tennessee and Georgia. Food City's holding company, K-VA-T Food Stores was privately owned, meaning any offtake deal inked with AquaMaof would probably not leak to the public. K-VA-T owned its own distribution center, meaning there would be no intermediaries between the Israeli company's loading dock at Richlands and a distribution network serving 123 outlets.

15 FOOD CITY SUPERMARKET AND HEADQUARTERS IN ABINGDON

VIAB also introduced Israeli executives to Tazewell County Council members who quickly pledged $1 million in tax abatements to the project. VIAB assisted in the submission of an application for a loan from the Virginia Coalfield Economic Development Authority to help finance the project. At the time VIAB estimated it would take $150 million "in public and private equity both from Israel and the U.S., as well as from private/public partnerships in the State and on Federal level."[149] VIAB also brought in Virginia Tech experts to produce assessments of the project.

No VIAB board member was more excited about Project Jonah than Chuck Lessin, the entrepreneurial lawyer involved in a portfolio of investments, ranging from bingo, to sports bars to fantasy sports gambling and even his own VIAB project. (See the chapter on Dominion Biofuels, LLC). In a December 5, 2013 VIAB board meeting he referred to Jonah urging VIAB to "think seriously about building a major project in Virginia," since according to Lessin Project Jonah could "create 426 jobs."

VIAB needed skilled support, so it hired consultant Lala Korall, and paid her company I-Deals LLC $11,788.82 from its 2014 budget in "management fees." Korall could spin out the right business speak and enticing numbers. The Harvard graduate majored in Economics and

---

[149] VIAB Board Meeting Minutes, December 5, 2013.

History, and later did an MBA at the Robert H. Smith School of Business at the University of Maryland. Korall assured the VIAB board that "for every job the aquaculture project will bring to the state, seven more are created through ancillary services like trucking, etc.—It is a vertical operation."[150]

On December 19, 2013 the Virginia Coalfield Economic Development Authority announced a loan of $10 million had been earmarked to Project Jonah, conditioned on their raising $137 million in matching funds.

The Virginia Coalfield Economic Development Authority was created by the state assembly in 1988 to diversify and grow the economy of southwest Virginia and bring jobs to a seven-county, one-city area. VCEDA is funded by local taxes paid by coal and natural gas companies. Its cornerstone program is a revolving low interest loan fund for land purchases, building acquisition, construction and equipment. VCEDA targets projects that can create at least 15 new full-time jobs within three years. Its website claims that between 1988 and 2016 it approved more than $188 million in funding for 289 projects across the coalfield region.

VCEDA set December 13, 2014 as the expiration date for the loan offer, so AquaMaof and VIAB had to move fast. Korall wasn't the only one on VIAB's "Project Jonah" payroll rushing to assemble the financing that would allow the project to take off. VIAB not only brought Virginia Tech, but in 2014 VIAB paid it $7,500 for "management services" from its then $176,000 budget.[151] Despite the effort, Project Jonah missed its 2014 deadline to meet the VCEDA performance agreement.

In January of 2015 VIAB dispatched a group of Tazewell County officials to visit AquaMaof's tilapia plant in Poland as part of "due diligence" activities. VIAB reported that it:

> ... took the group for visits including an on-site waste treatment plant that will work well in the Tazewell area as well as greenhouse companies and an aquaculture facility that is similar to the facility that we hope will be built in Virginia. Virginia's facility will be from 8 to 10 times larger. We also met with prospective venture capitalists.[152]

By September 17, 2015 the Tobacco Region Revitalization Commission, County of Tazewell and Dominion Aquaculture LLC signed a separate performance agreement for a $1.5 million grant. David Hazut,

---

[150] VIAB Board Meeting Minutes, December 5, 2013
[151] 2014 Audit Records of VIAB over travel reimbursement , as released under the Virginia Freedom of Information Act in MS Excel
https://Israellobby.org/viab2/FOIA/VA_Israel_Advisory_Board_2014.xlsx
[152] VIAB Board Meeting Minutes, March 24, 2015

CEO AquaMaof International LTD. signed an unconditional guarantee for "any and all obligations of every nature owing by Dominion Aquaculture, LLC." Lala Korall had moved up in the world, and was now listed in the documents as the contact to receive the $1.5 million at AquaMaof's U.S. subsidiary Dominion Aquaculture, LLC, housed in a dingy storefront building in Cedar Bluff, Virginia. But Project Jonah again missed 2014, 2015, then 2016 deadlines for the $10 million Virginia Coalfield Economic Development Authority loan.

16 PROJECT JONAH SITE SURROUNDING THE RICHLANDS WASTEWATER TREATMENT PLANT.[153]

A pattern of pleading for deadline changes from Project Jonah to Virginia Coalfield Economic Development Authority then commenced. All were quickly and perfunctorily granted. Then Project Jonah started hammering VCEDA to sweeten the terms of the loan. The Chief Operations Officer of Dominion Aquaculture, John H. Schiering, along with Lala Korall, who by August of 2017 was vice president of the venture, demanded and won a reduction of the required private matching funds to $110 million. The pair also demanded that VCEDA agree to convert portions of the loan to outright grants and reduce the interest rate to 0 percent until year three and 2.125 percent thereafter if certain performance benchmarks were met. VCEDA also quickly agreed to this, perhaps not realizing that they would not only forfeit $4.78 million of loan interest and

---

[153] Photograph by author taken in September of 2019.

principal repayments, but also only be repaid $6.46 million of their $10 million investment.[154]

TARGET: BLUE RIDGE AQUACULTURE

One core question raised by Project Jonah is why VIAB ever came to think of Richlands as a good location for a $100 million fish farm. A 360 degree geographic sweep of the region reveals that as in the case of Energix and Alony Hetz, Oran Safety Glass and Sabra, a proven market had already been established and was being served by savvy home grown American, and in this case, Virginia companies.

In Virginia it is no secret that Blue Ridge Aquaculture, located at almost the same latitude just 166 miles to the east of Project Jonah in Ridgeway, Virginia already revealed "proof of concept."

Blue Ridge Aquaculture (BRA) is the largest producer of Tilapia using recirculating aquaculture systems, producing four million pounds of tilapia and shipping 10-20 thousand pounds of live tilapia every day. BRA ships to Asian and Hispanic consumers in New York, Boston, Toronto and Washington D.C. who prefer live seafood over the packaged refrigerated or frozen kind. Blue Ridge Aquaculture's management believes they have won 20 percent of the market for live tilapia. BRA emerged in 1993 from a former catfish producer called Blue Ridge Fisheries that operated from 1988 through 1991. In 1993 BRA began producing tilapia, overcoming severe threats of disease with in-house technology, as well as pressing financial challenges.

As an employee owned company, BRA is socially conscious and believes "recirculating aquaculture systems are the most environmentally friendly, beneficial source of protein because of its relatively small ecological footprint."

AquaMaof's core technology is also recirculating aquaculture. In 2010 AquaMaof applied for a U.S. patent on a "modular aquaculture system" but its patent expired due to "Non Payment of Maintenance Fees." In 2014 AquaMaof again applied with partner Dakota Fisheries Inc. on behalf of the inventor Gary Myers of Sartell, Minnesota. On November 22, 2016, the trio was issued a patent number 9497941.

But it's not clear to industry observers that AquaMaof's technology is any better or substantially different than what is generally in use across the industry. On background they cite how the limited experience of workers at AquaMaof's showcase Poland facility caused it "not to work" properly and other problems at facilities in Russia. Fish farms are not gold mines,

---

[154] By the author's financial analysis.

and others looking into AquaMaof's numbers feel they simply "don't add up."

Late into Project Jonah, AquaMaof began claiming its Poland facility and proposed Virginia production site were not going to produce tilapia after all, but rather ship higher margin farm raised salmon. Although Virginia Coalfield Economic Development Authority reset the Project Jonah deadline once again for year-end 2019 in November of 2018, the state lender appeared to be starting to wriggle out of AquaMaof's net. The Virginia Coalfield Economic Development Authority demanded a copy of a signed MOU between Project Jonah and a local community college said to be poised to provide job training (to be lavishly funded by state Tobacco Commission grants not yet secured by AquaMaof, of course). VCEDA also demanded additional details on collateral, written evidence that the $110 million in private funds had been raised and a letter from the Virginia Economic Development Partnership that it fully supported the project.

Tazewell officials who already had put at least $1.5 million into Project Jonah soldiered on. In April of 2019 County Administrator Eric Young told the *Bluefield Daily Telegraph* that the facility was still, "very much in play…they are very close to having their money in place." Tazewell County Supervisor Mike Hymes claimed that although the initial plan was to raise tilapia, it may be changed to salmon. In any case, it would be different in that the idea now included "flash freezing" and taking the fish "directly to supermarkets."[155] This announcement calls into question whether an offtake agreement with Food City has either collapsed, since that proposed "offtake" partner is capable of shipping to its network of supermarkets. Or perhaps it was never signed in the first place.

While there are no signs that Project Jonah's investment bank 8F has secured funding for Project Jonah, surface ripples indicate something is moving. In 2019, Lala Korall reinvented herself once more, this time as the company's "Public Fundraising Director." Dominion Aquaculture Chief Operating Officer John H. Schiering forwarded to potential lenders a copy of a letter from the Tazewell County Tax Commissioner affirming the group had, in fact, acquired 123.09 acres "on the waters of the Clinch River in the Town of Richlands."

Once the massive operation is up and running, there is little doubt it will have to maximize profits to its Israeli and offshore investors. That means shipping flash frozen salmon direct to Food City and other

[155] Boothe, Charles, "Project Jonah moving forward: Tazewell officials still hard at work to make $130M fish farm happen" Bluefield Daily Telegraph, April 22, 2019, https://www.bdtonline.com/news/project-jonah-moving-forward-tazewell-officials-still-hard-at-work/article_cbc6fe16-649a-11e9-8172-176c31825789.html

supermarkets. AquaMaof will also need to take over all of Blue Ridge Aquaculture's live seafood markets on the East Coast. If it ever acquires private equity, Virginia's state-funding powered AquaMaof, like Sabra taking on Cedars (as profiled in the next chapter), will be well-positioned to undercut, underprice, out market and seize market share from one of Virginia's proudest, most innovative employee owned aquaculture operations.

17 SOUTHWEST VIRGINIA COMMUNITY COLLEGE IN RICHLANDS.

But Project Jonah may also now be a "zombie" like Charles Lessin's Appalachian Biofuels LLC after the crash in transportation fuel prices. Food City is stuffed to the gills with low-priced frozen tilapia sourced from Indonesia, a country that grows the fish with low price labor in conditions resembling flooded pits. There is also no shortage of frozen salmon at Food City, some ready for cooking on cedar planks, sourced from Florida.

Nevertheless, AquaMaof purchased an option to buy land adjacent to Southwest Virginia Community College. At the time of writing Project Jonah in partnership with the Virginia Economic Development Partnership was pressing the college to sign a memorandum of understanding to train aquaculture technicians for its future fish farming operations. Like Oran Safety Glass training, it is to be paid for by even more state-funded grants. SW has so far balked at signing the MOU, which will become "null and void" if the fish farm does not begin operations by year-end December 2020.

Is Project Jonah ready to swallow Blue Ridge Aquaculture? Will it use its new U.S. patents to pressure existing American fish farms for royalties? Or is it, like Charles Lessin, simply stalling for time and developing tactics to wriggle out of repaying Tobacco Commission grants?

9.
STATE SUBSIDIES BEHIND SABRA DIPPING COMPANY HUMMUS MARKET DOMINANCE

People of this country don't want some flash-in-the-pan hummus," said Sabra chairman Yehuda Pearl... "When it's 3 a.m., which hummus do Americans trust for their pita chip–dipping? Some new hummus that makes a lot of promises about taste, or a hummus with over 20 years' experience serving the American people? **The Onion**

In 2008 the satirical website *The Onion* published that "news" item titled "Sabra Hummus blasted rival Cedar's hummus Monday for lacking the ability, competence, and texture that Americans deserve from their hummus."

Like many stories from *The Onion*, the piece contained a disturbing kernel of truth. At that time, there was indeed a competition underway to become America's leading hummus brand between Cedar's and Sabra. At a deeper level, there is also an ideological battle about cultural appropriation as well as state subsidies and big business vs small private entrepreneurship in a growing market.

Hummus (alternatively hommus or houmous) is a chickpea (garbanzo bean) spread of blended olive oil, pureed sesame seeds, lemon juice, garlic and salt. Written recipes for Hummus originate in Cairo cookbooks from the 13th century.

The base ingredient of hummus, chickpeas, are great for a healthy diet. A one cup serving provides a high dose of fiber and protein along with minerals and vitamins. But they do not grow just anywhere. One reason hummus is popular among Palestinians and Jordanians is that all of the ingredients may be found in the garden or local market.

Chickpeas are a dryland crop. In the United States they are mostly grown in Montana (35 percent), Washington (32 percent) and Idaho (19 percent.) In 2017 the U.S. cultivated chickpeas on 6.2 million acres, with an average yield of 1,152 pounds per acre.[156] The U.S. could grow more, given sufficient market demand. Unfortunately for East Coast hummus producers, shipping from the drylands crop regions will continue to be a cost factor, unless research produces a more suitable variety (discussed later).

The U.S. market for hummus started slowly. In the mid-1980s Abe and Layla Hann, originally from Beirut Lebanon, started a small hummus and tabbouleh salad business in their kitchen for the local market 35 miles north of Boston. Their positive assessment of potential local market demand proved correct. Their products took off and the pair founded Cedar's Mediterranean Foods in Lawrence, Massachusetts. By 2005 the privately held company expanded to Haverhill with over 400 employees. Cedar's CEO claimed that the number of U.S. households with hummus in the refrigerator grew from 13 percent in 2013 to 24 percent in 2015.[157] He predicted 30 to 35 percent growth and the need to expand existing plant from 88,000 square feet to over a quarter million.

Cedar's namesake is the Lebanon cedar, which is displayed on the nation's flag, national airline and coat of arms. Lebanon has long been known as the "Land of Cedars." The legend traces further back than modern Lebanon. The ancient Mesopotamian poem the Epic of Gilgamesh describes the hero Gilgamesh and his companion Enkidu's mission to a legendary cedar forest. Some Babylonian versions of this early work of literature claim that cedar forest was located in "the Lebanon."

Sabra Dipping Company, like Cedar's, started out with branding tied to regional symbolism. Israeli born Zohar Norman established Sabra in New York with the fellow Israeli Yanko family in 1986. Yanko owned the "Tzabar" ("sabra" in Hebrew, which refers to a Jewish person born in pre-1948 Palestine) spreads and salad packaged goods brand in Israel. In 1994 the owner of Blue & White Foods, LLC purchased a 50 percent stake in Sabra. Blue & White refers to the Israeli flag, which was aligned with the company's business of distributing Israeli produced food in the U.S. Blue & White's owner Yehuda Pearl bought out Sabra's owners in 2002 and sold a majority stake to Israel's Strauss Group in 2005.

---

[156] "Chickpeas" Agricultural Marketing Resource Center, revised October 2018, https://www.agmrc.org/commodities-products/vegetables/chickpeas

[157] Killeen, Wendy, "Haverhill company spreads Mediterranean food across coasts" The Boston Globe, November 9, 2014 http://web.archive.org/web/20150328231923/https://www.bostonglobe.com/metro/regionals/north/2014/11/09/haverhill-company-spreads-mediterranean-food-from-coast-coast/ZGOYqaAwi9zzXEr7ctH0IJ/story.html

STRAUSS GROUP

Strauss Group founder Richard Strauss fled the Nazis to Palestine in 1936. He joined the Haganah organization which the British branded a terrorist outfit, to smuggle ammunition and push the English out of Palestine.[158] Strauss formed a dairy company to sell excess production from his 20 cows. Business grew, but also grew dependent on government subsidies. The company received Israeli government bailouts when it faltered in the 1950s.[159]

Strauss Group long traded on its support for the Israeli military, claiming on its website that:

> *Our connection with soldiers goes as far back as the country, and even further. We see a mission and need to continue to provide our soldiers with support, to enhance their quality of life and service conditions, and sweeten their special moments. We have adopted the Golani reconnaissance platoon for over 30 years and provide them with an ongoing variety of food products for their training or missions, and provide personal care packages for each soldier that completes the path. We have also adopted the Southern Shualei Shimshon troops from the Givati platoon with the goal of improving their service conditions and being there at the front to spoil them with our best products.*

The Golani Brigade has long been criticized for using Palestinian civilians, including children, as human shields, harassing Palestinians at checkpoints, collective punishment, ransacking homes and intimidation.[160] Strauss Group cultivated a joint venture in Israel which was led by Ronen Zohar in 1993. Zohar rose to become CEO of Strauss Frito-Lay (2000-2005) before being dispatched to the U.S. In 2008 Strauss inked a U.S. joint-venture with PepsiCo to distribute Sabra hummus. The success of this joint venture has now become central to VIAB's advice to Israeli companies that they partner with a U.S. company. "You can cut out 80

---

[158] Blankfeld, Keren, "Hummus Hullabaloo" Forbes, December 30, 2010 https://www.forbes.com/forbes/2011/0117/features-israel-strauss-group-sabra-hummus-hullabaloo.html#532b127d1694

[159] Blankfeld, Keren, "Hummus Hullabaloo" Forbes, December 30, 2010 https://www.forbes.com/forbes/2011/0117/features-israel-strauss-group-sabra-hummus-hullabaloo.html#532b127d1694

[160] Sherwood, Harriet "Former Israeli soldiers break the silence on military violations," the Guardian, May 6, 2011 https://www.theguardian.com/world/2011/may/16/former-israeli-soldiers-break-silence

percent of your cost factors with the right partner and probably time to money can increase five times."[161] To this day, Yehuda Pearl remains as partner and Chairman of the Board of Blue & White Foods which holds Sabra as its subsidiary company.

Given Strauss Group's history of seeking government support, it looked to Virginia for the biggest possible handout. Sabra's first dollop of taxpayer cash was delivered by Governor Tim Kaine who authorized $350,000 in seed funding from the Governor's Opportunity Fund at the Virginia Economic Development Program to finance a Sabra production facility.[162] The funding was based on matching funds from Chesterfield County where Sabra opened for business. Virginia also promised to cover the cost of job training to Sabra employees through VEDP's Job Investment Program.

According to market tracker Statista, Sabra's share of the U.S. market jumped from 17.3 percent in 2006 to 60.7 percent in 2015. Over the same period Cedar's fell from 15.8 percent to 4 percent.[163]

Unlike its partner PepsiCo, Sabra has never developed much of a taste for diversity among CEOs, who are invariably Israeli. In 2018 Tomer Harpaz replaced Shali Salit-Shoval, who returned to Israel. Shalit-Shoval replaced Ronen Zohar who became CEO after leaving the Strauss Frito-Lay joint venture in 2007.

In contrast, PepsiCo's CEO Indra Nooyi led the company from 2006-2018. The Indian American is ranked as one of the world's 100 most powerful women, and was courted to join Amazon's board of directors after leaving. Nooyi was replaced by Ramon Laguarta, born in Barcelona, Spain who became PepsiCo's sixth CEO. Laguarta, rose through the ranks from his start at a Spanish candy company through PepsiCo's European operations, overseeing acquisitions in Russia and handling complicated government affairs.

Sabra's demand for Virginia handouts is unending. In 2013 VIAB secured a $31,127 grant from the Tobacco Region Revitalization Commission for Virginia State University to establish chickpea production in Virginia through "on-farm research." This involved planting

---

[161] Hoch, Dov and Pomerantz, Sherwin, "US Financial Incentives for Israeli Companies" Presentation at the Israel American Business Summit, May 29, 2019

[162] Harris, Al, "Dipping into their options: How officials lured hummus maker to Va." Richmond BizSense, November 26, 2008. https://richmondbizsense.com/2008/11/26/dipping-into-their-options-how-officials-lured-hummus-maker-to-va/

[163]"Hummus dollar market share in the United States in 2006 and 2015, by brand" Statista, https://www.statista.com/statistics/441085/us-hummus-dollar-market-share-by-brand/

350 test plots in Virginia over a six year test period to identify the ideal "Sabra" chickpea.[164] In mid-2018 Sabra announced it wanted to expand its facility by 38,000 additional square feet, and began maneuvering for even more state funds and tax breaks.

2009 Location

Governor's Opportunity Fund - VEDP	$	350,000
Virginia Jobs Investment Program	$	50,000
Total	$	400,000

2012 Expansion

Commonwealth's Development Opportunity Fund	$	250,000
Virginia Jobs Investment Program Grant	$	83,250
Enterprise Zone Job Creation Grant (Estimated)	$	320,000
Chesterfield Opportunity Fund	$	200,000
Enterprise Zone 5 Year M&T Tax Grant (Estimated)	$	330,000
Waiver of Fees (Estimated)	$	51,900
Total	$	1,235,150

2013 Expansion

Commonwealth's Development Opportunity Fund	$	350,000
Virginia Investment Performance Grant	$	500,000
Virginia Jobs Investment Program	$	84,849
Enterprise Zone Job Creation Grant (Estimated)	$	40,000
Chesterfield Opportunity Fund	$	385,000
Enterprise Zone 5 Year M&T Tax Grant (Estimated)	$	687,500
Waiver of Fees (Estimated)	$	252,000
Total	$	2,299,349
Grand Total	**$**	**3,934,499**

18 SABRA DIPPING COMPANY – STRAUSS GROUP GOVERNMENT SUBSIDIES.

Entering the Sabra plant facility grounds, traveling down "Sabra Way" is like a border crossing between central American countries. There is a guard post hut with armed security. Present proper credentials, and the checkpoint gate is lifted. Fail to present a compelling case, and you can avail yourself of the large circular turnabout. On a small hill, two flags fly

---

[164] VIAB Board Meeting Minutes, December 5, 2013.

at equal height. The American flag, and the Sabra flag. In the distance rests a plant of impressive dimensions. But was the capital investment in the plant sufficient to meet the terms of Sabra's performance agreement for state funding? What about the promised numbers of full-time jobs? There is no way the public can find out.

SABRA'S PERFORMANCE AGREEMENT

The first few pages of Sabra's 2012 performance agreement with the providers of state funding seem serious. If Sabra did not generate its promised number of high-paying full-time jobs, or make a sufficient capital investment for plant expansion, it would have to return the funds. Chesterfield County and the Virginia Economic Development Partnership undertook the fiduciary obligation to audit Sabra. Sabra was required to annually provide "detailed verification reasonably satisfactory to the Locality, the Authority and VEDP of the Company's progress on the Targets."[165] But the performance agreement cuts out any potential public watchdog oversight or verification by predetermining that any tax payment information be entirely exempted from public disclosure.

Publicly released data received via the Virginia Freedom of Information Act is revealing, but not of performance. As the verification for capital investment, Sabra simply had The Dennis Group, a Sabra contractor and its designated food production factory builder, issue a series of two-line letters. In 2015 The Dennis Group certified that "the current committed capital investment for the Sabra Dipping Company's Project Obed for building and process equipment is $68 million." [166] The letter did not say the funds had been spent, placed in escrow, or anything final. In 2016, The Dennis Group was a bit less conditional, saying, "committed capital investment for the Sabra Dipping Company's Project Ruth for building and process equipment construction is $29 million." The figures from the letters were simply repeated in internal Virginia state documents closing out the $350,000 Governor's Opportunity Fund Grant. In other words, there was no independent certification or audit of capital investment by any disinterested third party.

For year 2013 certification of the "Governor's Opportunity Fund Grant Recipients" compliance of jobs creation, a mere notation from a Virginia Jobs Investment Program official was all that was needed. It read,

---

[165] "Governor's Development Opportunity Fund Grant, Chesterfield Opportunity Fund Grant" performance agreement executed by Sabra Dipping Company on June 5, 2012.
[166] The Dennis Group letters released by Chesterfield County.

"Per VJIP manager, all projected jobs covered under the FJIP agreement were disbursed by July 1, 2016."[167]

What the paper trail reveals is that none of the parties have any incentive to look too closely at what's going on, and so they don't. Auditing the performance agreement is a perfunctory effort undertaken by parties under no checks and balances.

MOU WITH VIRGINIA TECH

Thanks to VIAB, Strauss Group has already planted a flag at one of Virginia's leading educational innovators. This happened via a memorandum of understanding (MOU) with Virginia Polytechnic Institute and State University known as Virginia Tech. Virginia Tech offers 280 degrees and maintains a research portfolio of half a billion dollars, the only Virginia institution in the top fifty in terms of research expenditures. Virginia Tech serves 34,000 students at its main campus in Blacksburg, Virginia and facilities in six regions of the state as well as a branch in Switzerland.

Virginia Governor Terry McAuliffe visited Israel in summer of 2016. While there, the memorandum of Understanding was signed between Strauss Group (owner of the Sabra joint venture) and Virginia Tech. The governor held more than 20 high level meetings during his 46 hour tour. Were it not for the five donors accompanying the entourage to Israel (who have never been publicly named or included on news releases about the trip) the visit and MOU may well not have happened. According to Nathan Shor:

> *Getting those five donors to Israel, game changer, total game changer.*
>
> *In Ralph's [Robbin's] case, he worked for months to set up the meeting. We had a trip scheduled one time with McAuliffe. And it got cancelled. He had all these meetings set up. It got postponed for about 3 months. But try to get everybody's schedule back for all those meetings he had, he must have had half a dozen really high-level meetings for potential business to come to Virginia, or vice versa. Ralph had to get those all*

---

[167] Survey of Governor's Opportunity Fund Grant Recipients, released by Chesterfield County.

rescheduled. That's probably the worst part of his job is trying to schedule those trips. [168]

Never publicly released, the memorandum of understanding is lop-sided. Most of the tangible benefits accrue to Strauss Group. It also inserts VIAB into a position of greater influence over the Virginia Tech academic community research priorities. Prior to the MOU, this influence was informal, such as during the planning phase of Project Jonah when VIAB needed its authoritative rubber stamp of approval over its fish farm plan. VIAB had to pay for it. Post MOU, it seems unlikely VIAB will have to compensate Virginia Tech for access to its experts.

The MOU obligates Virginia Tech to support the commercialization of Strauss Group products in the U.S. market, without justifying why a land-grant university dependent upon state and federal funds should be working to guarantee the success of a foreign commercial enterprise. But at least Strauss flatters while at the same time being honest that it sees Virginia Tech as mostly a useful tool, rather than a partner, stating outright that:

> *WHEREAS Strauss, an F&B global [food and beverage] company, is a leader in food tech innovation, and Virginia Tech is a proven center of academic excellence and a connection to industry that supports a path to commercialization.[169]*

The first "ask" in the MOU is that Virginia Tech work to develop a variety of chickpea that can be successfully grown in Virginia's climate while meeting "pre-determined commercial requirements." It is also tasked to work on a "super smart greenhouse project in Southwest Virginia, a micro dairy facility and precision agriculture" though the relationship of these projects with Strauss business lines is not clarified. It may be that they are not at all related, other than being VIAB portfolio projects involving other Israeli companies. Indeed, in the MOU VIAB is identified as the very first entity that Virginia Tech should look to in "identifying potential projects" in a list that includes the Virginia Economic Development Partnership, Center for Innovative Technology, and other Virginia universities, and of course the Tobacco Commission and Virginia Coalfield Economic Development Authority.

---

[168] Hoch, Dov "What VIAB Does and How it Benefits Virginia," speech at the Weinstein Jewish Community Center, Richmond, VA, April 4, 2019. Introduction and remarks by former president of the Jewish Federation of Richmond Nathan Shor

[169] Virginia Tech Strauss Group Memorandum Of Understanding https://IsraelLobby.org/VIAB3/Strauss_Group_MOU_ocr.pdf

Virginia Tech is welcome to develop projects with Israel, but only one named entity is provided as a potential partner, the BIRD Foundation.[170] When Virginia Tech experts do go to Israel, their task is predetermined, according to the MOU, which says:

> *A Virginia Tech expert(s) can visit Israel on a yearly basis to meet with all of the candidates to select companies to invite to Virginia Tech for meetings that can include technical meetings, marketing meetings, consultations with other experts with the purpose to assist the company in developing and executing "market entry model" needed to enter the US market. The VIAB will be requested to assist with this program.*

The MOU is somewhat of a microcosm of the 1985 U.S. Israel Free Trade Area Agreement,[171] in which all of the market access and financial privileges accrue to mostly the Israeli side of the deal, and virtually nothing on the U.S. side.

Sabra is hungry for more state subsidies. Although not yet verifiable, it looks as though VIAB's code name for another round of state subsidies for Sabra's plant is "Vegan Non-Meat producer and Packager." Yehuda Pearl, the 49 percent Sabra Dipping Company stakeholder from Blue & White Foods has also developed a taste for Virginia State support, as we shall see in the case of UBQ in the next chapter.

---

[170] The Binational Industrial Research and Development (BIRD) Foundation was founded in 1977. It is jointly funded by the U.S. and Israel and has an endowment of $110 million.

[171] The cumulative U.S. bilateral trade deficit with Israel in goods since inception and adjusted for inflation is $182.25 billion. U.S. exporters continue to struggle for market access. See "U.S. Israel Free Trade Agreement Damage Assessment" IRmep, June 20, 2019
https://www.irmep.org/pdf/6202019ILFTA.pdf

10.
MAKING MORE WASTE OUT OF TRASH AT PROJECT RE-CYCLE MULTI-SITE

Virginia has been such a good friend to me personally and the company I work with. I would like to make every effort to have the new company in Virginia... I am sure you will find the proper way to encourage that... **Yehuda Pearl, Blue & White Foods**[172]

The United States produces so much plastic waste that for a long time it exported large amounts of it to China and Indonesia. China was particularly adept at creating a new industry of plastic recyclers to take in some seven million tons of plastic waste per year. There were synergies. On the West Coast, there were plenty of empty shipping containers that had delivered goods from China. With a growing domestic plastic recycling industry, Chinese brokers were happy to buy plastic trash to ship back across the Pacific Ocean for recycling.

But huge piles of U.S. plastic trash that was too tainted to recycle started piling up in landfills and being illegally dumped near China's east coast. So, in January of 2018 the Chinese government banned plastic waste imports. Shipments of plastic started going to South East Asian countries that had no ability to recycle it, so much of it is simply burned.[173]

Large amounts of the most valuable and easy to recycle plastic waste goes into the trash. That is because only 50 percent of Americans have an option to recycle that is as easy as simply throwing plastic away. So, the core U.S. problem is too much plastic trash, and too little culture of plastic recycling, which is a learned behavior that can be incentivized. The U.S. could handle more of its own plastic trash if Americans would recycle

---

[172] Martz, Michael, "Va. Showcases new Israeli technology, hope economic investment follows" Richmond Times-Dispatch, August 29, 2019
https://www.pressreader.com/usa/richmond-times-dispatch/20190829/281621012004557

[173]
https://www.npr.org/sections/goatsandsoda/2019/03/13/702501726/where-will-your-plastic-trash-go-now-that-china-doesnt-want-it

plastic waste accumulating in their homes. But that requires taking the time to sort out the plastic.

In Virginia, VIAB and its network think the opportunities created by this environmental crisis should go to Israel. Like other VIAB portfolio projects, heavy state subsidies and insider benefits framed the secret project from the beginning.

VIAB announced "Project Re-cycle Multi-site" in the following way in its 2018 annual report:

> *Multi-site Company recycles 95% of municipal waste and converts it to a new material that can be used for nearly every application plastic is used including building materials. The process eliminates the need for landfills. The company visited Virginia several times and is contemplating establishing its U.S. headquarter here as well as its first U.S. recycling facility. It will require several plants to serve the entire state. Expected jobs for HQ and initial plant 120 – 1-2 years.*

There was little need for code-name cloak and dagger. There is only one Israeli company claiming to be able to turn garbage into plastic.

The tiny plastic company is based in Kibbutz Tze'elim in the Negev desert. In 1947 Kibbutz Tze'elim was a tiny isolated, fenced outpost with plenty of flat terrain to host a military airstrip. That airstrip was a tiny bit of takeover infrastructure. Pilots flew out of Kibbutz Tze'elim to fight in Israel's 1948 War of Independence, triggering the Palestinian "Nakba" or "disaster" of displacement and ethnic cleansing.

Today Kibbutz Tze'elim is tiny, with a population of less than 500. The area is the beneficiary of considerable U.S. largesse demanded by Israel's U.S. lobby. For example, in 2005 the U.S. paid $45 million for Israel to build the Urban Warfare Training Center at the Tze'elim Army Base. The 7.4 square mile center trains U.S. army and UN peacekeepers. It was built because of unfinished business with the Palestinians. In 2005, the IDF wanted to hone its military capabilities against mostly defenseless Palestinians following the Second Intifada. The second Palestinian intifada, or "uprising" against Israel began in September of 2000 after Ariel Sharon toured the Temple Mount accompanied by a contingent of riot police. As expected, it touched off a deadly exchange.

Out of this enclave emerges UBQ, a company with less than 30 employees. It was founded in 2012 by Rabbi Yehuda Pearl and Jack Bigio. Pearl is the founder of the Sabra hummus brand. Bigio works in renewable energy. Unlike AquaMaof, UBQ does not appear to hold any U.S. patents for its allegedly revolutionary garbage to plastic process. But it does have high expectations for vast amounts of Virginia government support to launch its headquarters and manufacturing operations in Virginia.

In August of 2019 UBQ announced a new partnership with the Central Virginia Waste Management authority (CVWM). CVWM agreed to purchase 2,000 recycling bins, all with UBQ printed in prominent white lettering. CVWM will then distribute the bins for bottle, can and wastepaper recycling across the region. The bins were made, according to UBQ, with its proprietary garbage to plastic industrial process.

The deal follows a VIAB-funded junket to Israel that took state Senate Majority Leader Tom Norment and House Minority Leader Eileen Filler Corn to Israel in Spring of 2018. From Yehuda Pearl's perspective, it is now Norment's job to deliver state funding for UBQ to transfer its headquarters and a plant to Virginia. Pearl told Norment:

> *Virginia has been such a good friend to me personally and the company I work with. I would like to make every effort to have the new company in Virginia… I am sure you will find the proper way to encourage that…*

Norment was not randomly selected by VIAB for the junket or announcement. He sits on a special legislative subcommittee that decides the recipient and size of state financial incentives. UBQ CEO Jack "Tato" Bigio is asking for the not insignificant amount of $80 million for a plant he claims could create 250 jobs.

Will the gatekeepers to such capital, private and public, go for it?

A strict look at the market is not promising. Like most American states, Virginia's issue isn't creating more plastic. It's getting rid of and recycling the plastic it already has. That starts with getting more recycling bins (whether metal, wood or composite material) out to Virginians and incentivizing them to sort their recyclable plastic out of the waste stream.

The UBQ distributed bins are commodities. Virginia already has such bins, but what it needs most—like the rest of America, is a culture of recycling. It is also unclear whether UBQ actually possesses a cost-effective, revolutionary process for turning non-plastic waste into plastic. Could it, like other VIAB project with generic industrial processes, merely be attempting to break into Virginia's already established, but growing, plastic recycling industry? And if UBQ does have a revolutionary non-plastic waste to plastic conversion technology, is it competitive with existing petro-chemical plastic production? If not, will UBQ become reliant on taxpayer subsidies to operate a non-cost competitive plant? Virginians would do well to get clear answers to these questions.

11.
CONCLUSION – WHAT IS VIAB?

There's no state that has an agency that is funded by the state. There's [sic] probably 20 states that have some type of . . . Israel-America—Texas-Israel Chamber of Commerce, Southeast Region Association which is called Conexx. In Maryland they have a four-man team with at least ten times our budget that do this also, but it's nothing that's funded by the state. It's got a little bit of gravitas. But it doesn't have the gravitas if the state doesn't do anything about it. Can you imagine, I said to the Secretary of Commerce, now he's only been in the job six months . . . I said to him, do me a favor. Drive two hours. Sit with us for two hours. And drive two hours back. And he said, yes. Now, he understood and he cared. **Dov Hoch, Executive Director of the Virginia Israel Advisory Board**[174]

There is a major difference between the Virginia Israel Advisory Board's influence on the executive agencies of the state and the limited pressure that outside not-for-profit Israel chambers of commerce exert upon other state governments.

When a chamber of commerce petitions government for redress, there is a clear separation between its operation as an outside entity and the state government. Not so with VIAB. Members of the entities that created VIAB understand that. Nathan Shor, VIAB board member and past president of the Jewish Community Federation of Richmond, quipped:[175]

If he (Dov) was totally independent, he wouldn't be in the Pocahontas Building. He'd be working at Gather (co-working place) down the street trying to get his input into the board in

---

[174] Hoch, Dov "What VIAB Does and How it Benefits Virginia," speech at the Weinstein Jewish Community Center, Richmond, VA, April 4, 2019. Introduction and remarks by former president of the Jewish Federation of Richmond Nathan Shor

[175] Hoch, Dov "What VIAB Does and How it Benefits Virginia," speech at the Weinstein Jewish Community Center, Richmond, VA, April 4, 2019. Introduction and remarks by former president of the Jewish Federation of Richmond Nathan Shor

the Pocahontas Building on a regular basis, and that wouldn't work.

...we have an office on the floor with the senators in the Pocahontas building, so during session it's helpful and I think we have very informal, good relations with the people there, so we meet with some frequency.[176]

When VIAB convenes, all of the relevant players are there in the same board room, gathering side by side as fellow government agencies. The Office of Attorney General attends to provide an inoculating clearance of conflict of interest questions. Outside consultants seeking gigs can make their pitches. Entrepreneurs and venture capitalists wanting a piece of the action wade in. At the very moment they get down to the real business at hand, citing exceptions to the state's sunshine law that mean the rest won't be recorded in meeting minutes, the public's window into proceedings goes dark.

Lining up seed capital is as easy as walking down the street from the Pocahontas Building toward the capital and down to the left two blocks to the Tobacco Commission. On paper, the terms of grants are exacting and rigorous, and require payback in the event projects to not move forward. In reality, forgiveness in the event of failure is assumed. Virginians don't appear to want this.

A poll conducted September 25-October 30, 2018 by the Virginia Coalition for Human Rights asked 2,110 Virginians to agree or disagree with the following statement. "Since Virginia had a $500 million trade deficit with Israel in 2017, Virginia taxpayers SHOULD NOT continue to subsidize Israeli business projects in the Commonwealth."[177]

A plurality of Virginians 38.1 percent responded that they favored halting all taxpayer funding for Israeli business ventures, 32.7 percent of Virginians were neutral on the question, while 29.2 percent disagreed.

The Virginia Israel Advisory Board is a replicable model for how Israel can be inserted into the heart of state government. If it prevails in Virginia, it can be introduced into any state.

---

[176] Hoch, Dov "What VIAB Does and How it Benefits Virginia," speech at the Weinstein Jewish Community Center, Richmond, VA, April 4, 2019. Introduction and remarks by former president of the Jewish Federation of Richmond Nathan Shor

[177] Virginia Coalition on Human Rights, Virginia Poll on Taxpayer Subsidies for Israeli Companies, September 22, 2018. https://surveys.google.com/reporting/survey?hl=en&survey=cfrbeum2e6cbezo4hakmhleswa

The real purpose of VIAB is giving economic opportunities and political power to Israel, its board members and its extended community members. The public image VIAB wishes to cultivate is that it is building economic opportunities and jobs for all Virginians. But most of the benefits accrue only to Israel and a chosen few.

VIAB continually emits, publicly and privately, unsubstantiated claims about the economic returns on its projects that raise doubts among those closely tracking the numbers. When VIAB brazenly misrepresents what is happening, no government agencies are empowered to publicly call it out. There are no lasting institutional checks and balances restraining VIAB.

For example, VIAB claimed in its 2014 annual report that there were "no matters involving internal control and its operation necessary to bring to management's attention." In fact, during that very period, VIAB's habitual abuses of travel reimbursement policies were called into question, but not directly. The Auditor of Public Accounts performed an audit of the Division of Selected Agency Support Services (not VIAB) which was handling VIAB expense reimbursement when it was operating out of the governor's office.[178] It uncovered rampant abuses in VIAB's travel reimbursement—mostly requests for travel to Israel. Special policies were put in place to specifically stop VIAB's abuse, but they only lasted until VIAB reorganized under the legislative branch.

The taxpayer funded giveaways to Israel orchestrated by VIAB predicated on claims that jobs and tax revenues produce a return on state incentives. Although entities investing in VIAB's portfolio are legally empowered to verify job creation and tax generation metric compliance through their signed performance agreements, they simply don't do it.[179] Greensville County can't produce evidence of any independent verification of Oran Safety Glass performance metrics through its own data collection and monitoring. The same is mostly true in the case of Chesterfield County and Sabra Dipping Company. For the counties, simply not collecting or monitoring the data available under the performance agreement is safer than collecting it. Collecting it would imply oversight, and no county or Virginia state entity has any incentive or safety net if it were to try to oversee or perform checks and balances on

---

[178] Report on Audit, Division of Selected Agency Services for the year ended June 30, 2014, Commonwealth of Virginia
http://www.apa.virginia.gov/reports/DSAS2014.pdf

[179] The author requested evidence of performance agreement compliance monitoring from both counties. Chesterfield County produced limited information on performance agreement compliance. See https://IsraelLobby.org/Sabra Greensville County had no information on actual capital investment by Oran or job verification. See https://IsraelLobby.org/Oran

the projects of a hybrid political entity with the political power of VIAB and its extended community. Oversight could drive away other potential investors. It might alienate the Tobacco Commission. VIAB's self-propelled exit from gubernatorial oversight also demonstrates why. VIAB itself has far too much raw political power for checks and balances to function.

VIAB's culture of secrecy also has a corrosive impact on the state. When asked to comment on VIAB Vice Chairman Charles Lessin's secret list of VIAB projects, job creation and capital expenditures, the lead counsel of the Virginia Economic Development Partnership, Sandra McNinch, could not give a knowledgeable response. That is because it had either never seen the list and could not match the numbers to any project in its comprehensive database. The list was probably just another set of make-believe numbers produced to give the Tobacco Commission executive director cover for justifying his cancelation a $210,000 personal burden on Charles Lessin.

But the VIAB cult of secrecy not only enables such personal gains at the expense of state resources, also makes it impossible to quantify VIAB's long-term impact on the Virginia economy.

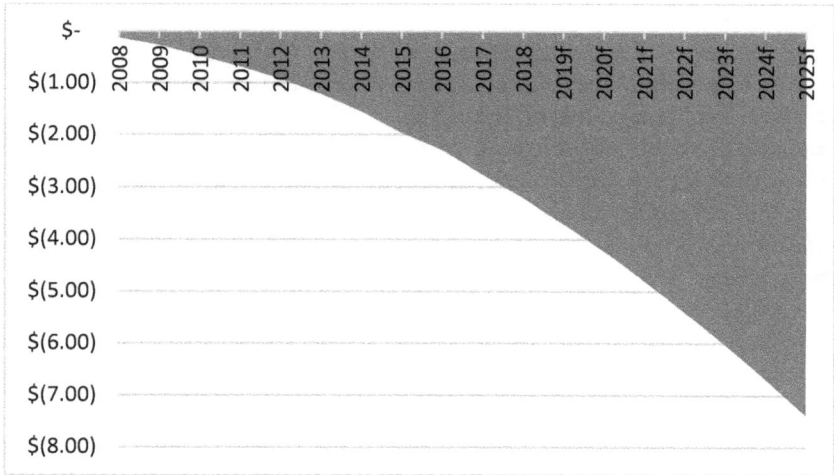

19 CUMULATIVE VIRGINIA TRADE DEFICIT IN GOODS WITH ISRAEL - ACTUAL AND FORECAST[180]

Over the past decade, Virginia's trade deficit with Israel has grown. In 2008 it was $128 million, by 2017 it was just under half a billion dollars.

---

[180] U.S. Census Division Statistics, forecast years are the author's own using arithmetic data regression.

Cumulatively, the negative impact of the unfavorable U.S. Israel Free Trade Area Agreement and VIAB's focused insertion of Israeli companies continually importing capital goods and other inputs will boost the overall deficit in goods from $3.2 billion in 2018 to a forecast $7.4 billion by 2025 if growth is only arithmetic, rather than geometric, which is unlikely.

Israel's exports of services, which could become even greater, won't even be measurable. Also, top line numbers from the Census Bureau international trade division data are misleading when it comes to goods trade with Israel. A large percentage of reported U.S. "exports" to Israel are in reality merely the return of unsold inventories of Israeli diamonds. In 2018 $4.7 billion in Israeli diamonds returned by the U.S. to Israel amounted to 34 percent of total U.S. "exports."

The Bureau of Economic Analysis is slow to generate "service" export figures and does not break them out at the state level. The figures consist of revenues produced in the U.S. from "majority owned" foreign companies, such as foreign airlines selling tickets to Americans. Under the advantageous terms of the FTA, Israel exported $7.4 billion in services to the U.S. while the U.S., a global services export leader, exported only $5.9 billion to Israel.[181]

Due to the way Israeli businesses are structured in Virginia, it is unlikely that they are even properly reported to BEA. Many Israeli joint ventures and foreign direct investments are channeled through offshore banking centers for tax and other purposes. Though the ultimately beneficial owner of Sun Tribe Solar is certainly Energix and Alony Hetz, there are almost certainly now, or soon will be, other intermediaries, on paper at least, running the operation through offshore banking centers. BEA is incapable of accurately deriving service export data from such corporate structures. So, Sun Tribe Solar, on paper and in the eyes of the public and of all relevant data collectors and regulators, will continue to be just another home grown Virginia based company, producing jobs, generating revenues and returning benefits to the state. This is an entirely false picture. And this is the challenge presented by VIAB. It is a deceptive enterprise set up to mask its truly harmful purpose. It all begins with the entity's name.

An advisory board is a body that provides non-binding strategic advice to the management of a corporation, organization, or foundation. It is established by the beneficiary of its advice to accomplish objectives derived from its mission. Real advisory boards have many advantages. The informal nature of an advisory board lends greater flexibility in structure

[181] "Israel: U.S.-Israel Trade Facts" Office of the U.S. Trade Representative, https://ustr.gov/countries-regions/europe-middle-east/middle-east/north-africa/israel#targetText=U.S.%20goods%20exports%20to%20Israel,1985%20(pre%2DFTA).

and management compared to an organization's board of directors. Unlike a private sector or nonprofit board of directors, a typical advisory board does not have the authority to vote on corporate matters or bear legal fiduciary responsibilities. Many new or small businesses choose to have advisory boards in order to benefit from the knowledge of others, without the expense or formality of the board of directors.

VIAB exists because Jewish federations lobbied to bring it into existence. They created VIAB, because they wanted it, and Israel needed it. VIAB therefore is presently inside Virginia's state government, not because citizens of the Commonwealth or the private sector needs Israeli corporate (and indirectly Israeli) involvement in their state. To the contrary, the needs of Israel, its lobby and its private sector necessitate their involvement in receptive U.S. states.

If the office of the governor truly needed foreign state involvement in developing Virginia's economy, he would not have needed the ongoing intervention of Jewish federations to accomplish it. However, left to his own devices, he would have likely looked to economic development powerhouses first, such as China or Germany, to sit on a board to advise him. The first advisory board was created centered around Israel due to the political power and machinations of the Jewish federations. Not the needs of the state.

This is the very same trajectory of the U.S. Israel Free Trade Area Agreement. Upon notification in 1984 that the U.S. was going to enter "negotiations" to bring about a beneficial and duty free trading relationship with Israel, industry stakeholders questioned the premise of the move. In filings opposing the FTA, many questioned why the Reagan administration was pushing a deal with Israel, a tiny market with little to nothing to offer in reciprocity, rather than a larger market with more to offer. Even Thomas Gossage, Group Vice President of Monsanto, questioned the deal on these terms in a letter to the International Trade Commission:

> *Our government should make the distinction between the advanced developing and developed countries with a strong current account position (such as Taiwan, Hong Kong and Japan) and those with severe balance of payments problems...*[182]

In 1984-1985 although 76 major U.S. industry and educational groups stood opposed to the FTA with Israel, including the AFL-CIO, University

---

[182] Thomas Gossage letter to Secretary Kenneth Mason, U.S. International Trade Commission, May 2, 1984. AIPAC, Espionage and the US-Israel Free Trade Agreement, Israel Lobby Archive, https://IsraelLobby.org/FTA/Monsanto/default.asp

of California and Hunt-Wesson Foods, they obviously were not devoted full-time to opposing the deal, with 100 percent of their efforts. The Israel affinity organizations including AIPAC and the American Israel Chamber of Commerce and Industry were 100 percent devoted. Alongside a list of low profile commercial entities such as King Super Markets and The Paul Rogers Company, just 17 entities, backed by the Israel lobby, prevailed in getting the FTA passed by congress and signed into law. Despite the theft of an International Trade Commission report containing all the proprietary industry and market data of FTA opponents, and its handling and distribution by AIPAC and the Israeli Ministry of Economics, which was investigated by the FBI, no public interest, law enforcement initiative or economic argument had any impact.

Since U.S. states cannot sign meaningful bilateral trade agreements, Israel partisans in Virginia cannot pass a bilateral trade and investment agreement with Israel. So, they've done the next best thing. But what have they created, if it is not an advisory board? Is it an economic development board?

No. An economic development board is a government agency for planning and executing strategies to enhance a state's position as a state, regional or global business center and to grow the economy. It is responsible for designing and delivering solutions that create value for investors and companies within the stated geographical area. In this way, for states, they seek to create economic opportunities and jobs for the people of the state and help shape the state's economic future.

Virginia already has an economic development board called the Virginia Economic Development Partnership. It is the entity that in 2019 successfully lured Amazon into the state with the hope of creating 25,000 jobs over the next 20 years. Though created around the same time as VIAB, the Virginia Economic Development Partnership's mission is broadly to encourage, stimulate, and support development and expansion of the Commonwealth's economy. It has offices in Germany, Japan, and South Korea because those are countries with high economic relevance to the state, not because VEDP is staffed with or surrounded by partisan entities hoping to channel 100 percent of their deals to a single foreign country. One of VEDP's key roles is coordination and strategy to create new businesses and grow existing businesses. This expands the total number of jobs and results in a rising average wage.

VIAB performs activities that are the opposite of an economic development board's mandate. Rather than shop around for international opportunities that complement state strategy or industrial development needs, it claims it is self-evident that just about any company from Israel is an innovative industry leader with something to offer the U.S.—when they are mostly nothing of the sort. It then deploys political muscle, cronyism, networking, self-dealing, secrecy and non-coordination to push through the deals. In fact, VIAB appears to do the opposite of coordination, that is, increasing net total employment through awareness of existing Virginia industries. In the case of Project Jonah, it appears VIAB's intention is to replace an established industry, and channel the profits to Israel. VIAB also seeks to channel any opportunities to build the talent base to members of its own community in the form of plum management, consulting and ownership stakes.

When Senator Ryan McDougle proposed that VIAB be merged into the state economic development board, the VEDP, under his substitute bill (see the appendix) VIAB's executive director would have been appointed by VEDP, and its staff would have worked on projects. VIAB was strongly opposed. As Nathan Shor summarized it, discussing VIAB's move out the Governor's office:

But, they wanted to make us state appointees, but it would have been a worthless job at that point, because then you're turning over every four years, and then why point out a big donor who may have no connection to Israel, you have got to have this connection, you've got to be able to pick up the phone like Ralph did, like Dov does, to get to those right decision makers.[183]

In Shor's view, big donors could not have been as easily deployed to push through deals if VIAB functioned more like a bona fide government agency. But merging VIAB into VEDP would have had a positive impact on corruption. It is hard to see VEDP staff accepting or signing off on Charles Lessin's sweetheart deal with the Tobacco Commission. Full time, paid government staff aren't allowed to act that way. Unfortunately, VIAB's "eat what you kill" board member compensation system encourages such dealings, to the point that board members who are either participating in or could share the upside benefits of VIAB's portfolio feel sorrow for the VIAB executive director's compensation as a salaried employee. Again, according to Nathan Shor:

He's [Dov Hoch] served Israelis and Americans alike in China [and] all around the world. You know this is a state

[183] Hoch, Dov "What VIAB Does and How it Benefits Virginia," speech at the Weinstein Jewish Community Center, Richmond, VA, April 4, 2019. Introduction and remarks by former president of the Jewish Federation of Richmond Nathan Shor

*agency job. It's not a high paying job. It's not a benefits-full job
to go out there, you know, and eat what you kill so to speak.*[184]

VIAB is a "cat's paw" with a long tail trailing behind it. Economic development boards don't operate that way. The four-year turnover Shor cites as a deficiency is actually check and balance that ensures clean government. Again, it is the complete opposite of VIAB, where many board members such as Mel Chaskin, Charles Lessin and Nathan Shor have been active for many more years, as Shor readily admits:

> *I've been fortunate enough to be on the board now for VIAB
> for about six years, because I was the president of the (Jewish
> Community) Federation (of Richmond) I went in and I've been
> able to stay on the board. There has been some really exciting
> stuff that VIAB has been able to pull off over the years…*

Legitimate economic development boards also take pains to encourage research and development in local universities. If one only reads announcements about the MOU (and not the text within the MOU itself), one might think that was the point of the Strauss Group Sabra MOU with Virginia Tech. But close inspection again reveals the opposite.

The MOU places Virginia Tech into the role of an order taker, rather than innovator. It is supposed to labor locally and nationally to create the markets Sabra and Strauss Group need to expand. Virginia Tech only gets the scraps from Strauss Group's table. Its dairy and chickpea research and development in Israel would not be practical in Israel, with its vastly different climate. So, it is farming that out through Virginia Tech. But the MOU makes clear that any true innovation will continue to take place, be patented by and be proprietary to, Strauss Group and not Virginia Tech. The MOU will over the long term compete with and diminish the size of Virginia Tech's own research and development portfolio and patents.

VIAB's direct and indirect contacts with institutions of higher learning in Virginia also have a chilling effect. If Southwest Virginia Community College doesn't want to play ball as "Project Jonah's" training center, will VIAB work to punish it by having its budget cut? Should such fears even be part of the equation?

So, is VIAB a chamber of commerce? A chamber of commerce (or board of trade) is a form of business network, for example, a local

---

[184] Hoch, Dov "What VIAB Does and How it Benefits Virginia," speech at the Weinstein Jewish Community Center, Richmond, VA, April 4, 2019. Introduction and remarks by former president of the Jewish Federation of Richmond Nathan Shor

organization of businesses whose goal is to further the local interests of businesses.

Business owners in towns, cities and sometimes regions form these local societies to advocate on behalf of the business community. Businesses within the declared geographical confines make up the members and they elect a board of directors or executive council to set policy for the chamber. The board or council then hires a president, CEO or executive director, plus staffing appropriate to the size of the operation, to run the organization.

The U.S. Chamber of Commerce is probably one of the best known chambers in America due to its size and visibility. It lobbies Congress on behalf of American businesses and has been around since 1912. City and state chambers of commerce have been around a long time as well. The Charleston Chamber of Commerce in South Carolina traces its existence back to colonial times in 1773.

VIAB clearly is not a chamber of commerce. Although it claims to want to provide jobs and build the tax base in Virginia, its primary focus is on bringing foreign, in this case Israeli, companies into Virginia. That means it does not fit the category.

Neither, should it be added, do most Israel-focused U.S. organizations that actually call themselves Chambers of Commerce fit inside the chamber mold. Most, like the Texas chamber VIAB's executive director once led, focus on creating opportunities for Israeli companies and their Israel advocacy community members rather than a U.S. region. They try to frame their work as beneficial in the same way that VIAB does, but many of their activities upon close examination look to be mostly Israeli-serving and self-serving.

If VIAB is not an advisory board, not an economic development board, and not a chamber of commerce, what precisely is it? The answer becomes clearer not only from this book's exploration of VIAB's actual activities, but also VIAB's continually evolving website, which now states:

> The Virginia Israel Advisory Board (VIAB) is a government agency that helps Israeli companies build and grow their U.S. operations in Virginia.[185]

Israel has limited sales potential in its domestic market because it is a small country. Israel also has limited regional export potential because of the way it came into being and international relations. Massive—though long-denied—ethnic cleansing before and during its "War of Independence" followed by ongoing repression of Palestinians have made

---

[185] Consulted October 13, 2019

its products and services anathema among neighboring country consumers.

Despite the ongoing hype of being a "start-up nation," Israel cannot compete with major research centers of innovation such as Silicon Valley as a developer of intellectual property. But it can use its single overriding comparative advantage to promote its exports and foreign direct investment.

Intel, Microsoft, Google and others have created thousands of high paying jobs and invested billions in venture capital in Israel. It cannot be seriously argued that Israel's high-tech industries are primarily the result of Israeli research and development. Like its clandestine nuclear weapons production infrastructure, it is heavily reliant on the mass importation of foreign know-how, capital and materials. That foreign investment could have gone to Asia or Europe. It wound up in Israel for the same reason Israel's companies are entering Virginia.

When countries strategize to increase exports and foreign direct investments, they focus intensely on their comparative advantages. That is, their ability to carry out a particular activity more efficiently than another. The government entities and domestic nonprofits that perform the role "in-country" are known as export and foreign direct investment promotion councils. In that sense, VIAB most closely represents an Israeli export promotion council. With one twist. It has, like a cowbird laying its eggs in the nest of another species, managed to externalize completely the council's operation costs while selling the switch as of great benefit or equal value to the unsuspecting parents.

Israel's true comparative advantage is unlike any other country in the world. As applied to Virginia, it is clearly not that an Israeli company can make better hummus than any U.S. firm. AquaMaof's recirculating aquaculture technology, patents and all, is not technologically superior enough alone to destroy Blue Ridge Aquaculture. It takes more than that.

As already demonstrated, Oran Safety Glass was given the secret recipe to make the Army's top secret armored glass. Its own products were not initially acceptable to the Pentagon. The same goes for the trendy front company for Alony Hetz and Energix. Sun Tribe Solar LLC's comparative advantage does not lie in solar energy equipment, savvy project management, or even its marketing hype. The same is also true for UBQ's transparently silly plan to add to the plastic waste stream by producing ever more plastic out of garbage. Yehuda Pearl's demand for government support seems to almost intentionally hammer home the comparative advantage that he's really leveraging.

VIAB's activities in Virginia will produce billions in revenues for Israel and millions for VIAB insiders. As illustrated in the chapter about Sun Tribe Solar and other chapters, the highest end, highest value knowledge worker jobs will be staffed by Israelis and the chosen few from VIAB's extended ecosystem. Lala Korall, upon reflection, might more accurately characterize VIAB, and not Project Jonah, as the real "vertical operation."

These case studies in Virginia expose and documents a simple truth. The state Israel advocacy ecosystem—the Israel lobby in Virginia—has built a new mechanism for self-dealing in order to build its own—and Israel's—economic and political power. It is milking state taxpayers and pools of state funding on entirely false pretenses. It is an integrated strategy from the name it has given itself to the regular reports of inflated estimates of its economic contribution. It has bypassed the legislative process, because it could not win funding for such projects on their own merits if mitigated by even extremely flawed government representation of the populace. When VIAB negotiates funding to be signed off by counties, increasingly all relevant aspects of the relevant meetings are closed to the public.[186] It is only after skimming off most of the cream churned from its projects and channeling it to insiders, that the milk is touted to the taxpaying public as a new and essential boost to the state's economic health. VIAB is unaccountable to job loss or the bankruptcy of bystander Virginia companies.

In summary, Israel's key comparative advantage in Virginia is its small group of highly educated, savvy, interconnected and extremely active Israel advocates. They are willing to do whatever it takes to advance their cause, and furiously fight any who meaningfully challenge their activities. They are not trying to seize market share from American and Virginia companies because they are evil. They are not debasing the fiduciary responsibilities of the Tobacco Commission because such debasement is their primary objective. They do not continually "lead on" Tazewell County economic development officials just to avoid repaying $1.5 million in free grant money—although this money will almost certainly never be repaid. The crookedly lopsided Sun Tribe Solar contracts foisted on public schools are not made purely as predatory rent-seeking. They are also not moving around their government organization, either from the governor's office to the legislature or into Virginia Tech, purely as a show of force.

No. They are doing all this for Israel and to politically empower their own community. They are trying to do it in a way that hides the extensive

---

[186] For example, Sabra Dipping Company is now seeking funds to expand. The Chesterfield County Economic Development Authority has elevated to the highest level the art of "preemptively closed to the public and sunshine law" meetings on the matter. See
https://www.chesterfield.gov/AgendaCenter/Economic-Development-Authority-14

self-dealing and lack of any great benefit to outsiders.[187] They are doing it in a way that insulates and protects Israel from any consequences for its human rights record by human rights campaigners and others concerned about Middle East policy. When similar—but by no means the same—strategies were attempted on a much smaller scale by advocates for trade and normal relations with apartheid South Africa, they failed. So far, Israel and its advocates are succeeding.

Most members of the VIAB, Jewish federations and broader Israel advocacy ecosystem are American citizens and have an inherent right as Americans to advocate for whatever cause they wish. But they don't have the right to do it as a government agency, cloaking its activities in secrecy, engaging in constant self-dealing and selling it all to the public on false pretexts. That is why Virginians, including many of the Jewish faith, should ramp up their work as state human rights advocates to further expose and challenge VIAB.

This book makes the case that VIAB is an inherently conflicted government agency engaged in corrupt dealings, that should be permanently abolished. Americans from other states should work to ensure that VIAB equivalents are not sprouting up in their midst. If other hybrids are engaged in self-dealing on false pretexts, and extracting unwarranted state support empowered by self-dealing, they too should be shut down. The cost of such cronyism is far too high.

---

[187] VIAB seems to have severely underestimated the Virginia Freedom of Information Act's potential to expose its operation. It is now nearly impossible to research and obtain government files about the operations of national Israel advocacy organizations such as the American Israel Public Affairs Committee as completely and efficiently under the Freedom of Information Act due to legal precedents which have rendered impotent the federal sunshine law.

APPENDIX

VIAB BOARD MEMBERSHIP AND SERVICE[188]

First Name	Last Name	Location/Org	Service
George F.	Allen	Midlothian	2005-2008
Samuel H.	Asher	Jewish Community Federation of Richmond	2012-2013
Tommy P.	Baer	Midlothian	2007-2010
Sandra L.	Barmak	Fairfax Station	2005-2010
Kenny F.	Barnard	Amelia	2010-2012
Gayle F.	Barts	Sutherlin	2010-2011
Michael J.	Blachman	Portsmouth	2005-2014
Peter	Blake	Portsmouth	2005-2014
Irving M.	Blank	Richmond	2005-2018
Lane	Brent	Forsythe	2006-2008
Mark	Broklawski	Fredericksburg	2015-2018
Jeffrey	Brooke	Virginia Beach	2008-2018
Richard	Brown	Secretary of Finance	2010-2012
Delegate Kathy J.	Byron	Lynchburg	2010-2012
John	Cannon	South Boston	2010-2012
Diana F.	Cantor	Richmond	2005-2008
Jerome Ian	Chapman	Alexandria	2016-2018
Mel	Chaskin,	Clifton	2005-2018
Jim	Cheng	Secretary of Commerce and Trade	2010-2014
David R.	Cundiff	Penhook	2010-2012
Joshua M.	David	Newport News	2005-2017

---

[188] Source: Annual "Bluebooks" from the Secretary of the Commonwealth. https://www.commonwealth.virginia.gov/va-government/bluebook-reports/

Larry	Davidson	Roanoke	2015-2018
Israel	Dean O'Quinn	Bristol	2010-2012
Debra N.	Diener	Arlington	2008-2010
Linda	DiYorio	Wytheville	2010-2012
Mark B.	Dreyfus	Virginia Beach	2005-2018
Maya M.	Eckstein	Richmond	2009-2014
Craig	Einhorn		2012-2014
The Honorable Eileen	Filler-Corn	Springfield	2015-2018
Frances	Fisher	Fairfax	2006-2017
Laura	Fornash	Secretary of Education	2012-2014
Will	Frank	Henrico	2015-2018
Alan M.	Frieden	Virginia Beach	2005-2008
Aviva	Frye	Bristol	2015-2018
Michael C.	Gelman	Jewish Community Federation of Greater Washington	2005-2010
Michael	Gillette	Lynchburg	2005-2018
Michael E.	Ginsberg	Arlington	2012-2014
Ronald A.	Glaser		2012-2014
Scott	Goodman	Charlottesville	2005-2006
Patrick O.	Gottschalk	Secretary of Commerce and Trade	2006-2010
Paul H.	Grossman	Richmond	2012-2014
Jeffrey H.	Gumenick	Richmond	2005-2009
Burgess	Hamlet	Basset	2010-2012
Scott M.	Harwood	Farmville	2010-2012
Charles R.	Hawkins	Chatham	2010-2011
Todd	Haymore	Secretary of Agriculture and Forestry	2010-2017
Loren W.	Hershey	Oakton	2005-2006
Sophie R.	Hoffman	Fairfax Station	2005-2018
Anne	Holton	Secretary of Education	2015-2016
Todd R.	House	Falls Church	2005-2014
Jay M.	Ipson	Richmond	2012-2014

Karen	Jaffe	Norfolk	2007-2010
Jordon M.	Jenkins Jr	Blackstone	2010-2011
Delegate Joseph P.	Johnson Jr.	Washington	2010-2012
Maurice A.	Jones	Secretary of Commerce and Trade	2015-2016
Joel	Kanter	Vienna	2012-2018
Stewart	Kasen	Jewish Community Federation of Richmond	2005-2010
William J.	Kilberg	McLean	2012-2014
Delegate Terry G.	Kilgore	Gate City	2010-2012
Jay, President,	Klebanoff	United Jewish Federation of Tidewater	2015-2018
Larry	Krakover	Burke	2005-2018
Stuart S.	Kurlander	Jewish Community Federation of Greater Washington	2012-2014
Roy	Lasris	United Jewish Community of The Virginia Peninsula, Inc	2005-2010
Charles	Lessin	Richmond	2012-2018
Delegate Daniel W.	Marshall, III		2010-2012
Stephen H.	Martin	Chesterfield	2005-2006
Delegate Donald W.	Merricks	Chatham	2010-2012
H. Ronnie	Montgomery	Jonesville	2010-2012
Harrison A.	Moody	Blackstone	2010-2011
Abby	Moore	Richmond	2015-2018
Thomas R.	Morris	Secretary of Education	2006-2010
Sandra F.	Moss	Dillwyn	2011-2012
Arlene	Murphy	Roanoke	2005-2007
Jay	Myerson	Reston	2012-2018
Sherman L.	Naidorf	Annandale	2005-2008
Amy P.	Nisenson	Richmond	2005-2014
Connie	Nyholm	Alton	2010-2012
Kevin	O'Holleran	Richmond	2015-2018

David A.	Oblon	Arlington	2012-2017
Edward	Owens	South Boston	2010-2012
Timothy	Powers	Lovettsville	2012-2016
Senator Phillip P.	Puckett	Russell	2010-2012
David S.	Redwine	Gate City	2010-2012
Kenneth O.	Reynolds	Abingdon	2010-2012
Senator William Roscoe	Reynolds	Martinsville	2010-2012
Aaron	Roberts	Cedar Bluff	2012-2018
Neal, President	Rosenbaum	United Jewish Community of The Virginia Peninsula	2015-2016
Senator Frank M.	Ruff, Jr.	Mecklenburg	2010-2012
Annabel	Sachs	United Jewish Federation of Tidewater	2005-2010
Richard, President	Samet	Jewish Community Federation of Richmond	2015-2016
Jody, President	Sarfan	United Jewish Community of The Virginia Peninsula	2016-2018
Joyce Slavin	Scher	Richmond	2015-2016
Michael J.	Schewel		2005-2006
Nannette, President	Shor	Jewish Community Federation of Richmond	2016-2018
Nathan	Shor	Richmond	2015-2018
Samuel A.	Simon	McLean	2009-2014
Mark	Sisisky	Richmond	2006-2010
Steven	Skaist		2017-2018
Jordan	Slone	Norfolk	2005-2009
Robert	Spiers	Stony Creek	2011-2012
John M.	Stallard	Nnicksville	2010-2012
Scott	Stein	United Jewish Community of The Virginia Peninsula, Inc.	2012-2014
Stephen David	Stone	Alexandria	2005-2006

Julie Alexa	Strauss		2017-2018
David	Tenzer	Roanoke	2005-2018
Cindy M.	Thomas	South Hill	2010-2012
Patricia S.	Ticer	Alexandria	2008-2010
Dietra	Trent	Secretary of Education	2016-2017
Steven	Valdez	Richmond	2016-2018
Gary D.	Walker	Charlotte Court House	2011-2012
Alvin President	Wall	United Jewish Federation of Tidewater	2012-2014
Senator William C.	Wampler Jr.	Bristol	2010-2012
Marcus M.	Weinstein	Richmond	2008-2018
Delegate Thomas C.	Wright, Jr.	Victoria	2010-2012
Robert, President	Zahler	Jewish Community Federation of Greater Washington	2015-2018
Kenneth R.	Zaslav	Richmond	2005-2009
Suzan F.	Zimmerman	McLean	2005-2009

VIAB BOARD MEMBER APPOINTMENT AND TOTAL VIRGINIA CAMPAIGN CONTRIBUTIONS

Appointment by	VIAB Board Member	Amount
House	Marcus M Weinstein	$293,050
Designated Member	Michael J Schewel	$156,828
Governor	H Ronnie Montgomery	$96,116
House	Mel Chaskin,	$77,640
Governor	Loren W Hershey	$73,360
House	M Scott Goodman	$69,500
Governor	Karen G Jaffe	$65,149
Designated Member	Patrick O Gottschalk	$62,564
Governor	William J Kilberg	$62,088
Governor	Samuel A Simon	$57,423
Governor	Mark B Sisisky	$53,150
Governor	Jay M Ipson	$48,037
Governor	Charles Lessin	$40,293
Governor	Roscoe Reynolds	$27,625
Governor	Jerome I Chapman	$25,530
House	Jordan E Slone	$24,000
Governor	Jeffrey H Gumenick	$22,123
Governor	Eileen Filler-Corn	$22,100
Senate	Steven David Stone	$18,642
Governor	Kenneth R Zaslav	$15,900
Governor	Michael J Blachman	$15,467
House	Tommy Wright	$14,580
Governor	Charles R Hawkins	$14,433
House	Terry Kilgore	$13,744
Jewish Community Federation	Richard S Samet	$12,940
Governor	Maya Eckstein	$12,915
Governor	Michael E Ginsberg	$12,351
Senate	Patsy Ticer	$11,212
Governor	Scott M Harwood	$8,918
Governor	Sophie R Hoffman	$8,736
Governor	Connie Lee Nyholm	$7,750
Senate	Frank Ruff	$6,851

Governor	Debra N Diener	$5,600
Jewish Community Federation	Stewart M Kasen	$5,600
Senate	Joel Stephen Kanter	$5,150
Governor	Tommy P. Baer	$5,100
Senate	William Wampler, Jr	$5,000
Jewish Community Federation	Neal A Rosenbaum	$4,825
Governor	Alan M Frieden	$4,650
Jewish Community Federation	Stuart S Kurlander	$4,600
Senate	George F. Allen	$3,847
Senate	Jeffrey F Brooke	$3,625
Governor	Joshua M David	$2,928
Governor	Marc Broklawski	$2,860
Governor	Todd R House	$2,182
House	Larry Krakover	$2,180
Governor	Arlene Murphy	$2,000
Designated Member	Anne Holton	$1,850
Governor	Burgess Hamlet	$1,750
Senate	Steve Martin	$1,700
Governor	Linda P DiYorio	$1,645
Jewish Community Federation	Alvin A Wall	$1,500
Governor	Irving M Blank	$1,480
Senate	Abby Moore	$1,475
Governor	William R Frank	$985
Senate	H Lawrence Davidson	$850
Governor	Timothy Powers	$800
Designated Member	Laura W Fornash	$756
Governor	Aviva Frye	$696
House	Fran Fisher	$675
Governor	Sandra L. Barmak	$618
Designated Member	Jim Cheng	$500
Governor	Gayle F Barts	$350
Senate	Diana F Cantor	$250
Governor	Harrison A Moody	$250
Governor	John Stallard	$250
House	Julie A Strauss	$208

Governor	David Redwine	$200
Governor	J M Jenkins, Jr	$200
House	David A Oblon	$150
Governor	Steven Valdez	$150
Governor	Kenneth O Reynolds	$125
Governor	Robert H Spiers, Jr	$125
Jewish Community Federation	Robert E Zahler	$125
Jewish Community Federation	Samuel H. Asher	$118
Designated Member	Peter Alan Blake	$65
	Total	$1,531,008

JEWISH FEDERATIONS RECOMMEND CHANGES TO VIRGINIA STATE TEXTBOOKS

Jewish Community Federation
OF RICHMOND

Nannette Shor
President
Ellen Renee Adams
President Elect
Stuart C. Siegel
Vice President
Seth Kaplan
Vice President &
General Campaign Chair
Richard A. Arenstein
Jerome Gumenick
Nelson J. November
Mark B. Sisisky
Honorary Vice Presidents
Frances Goldman
Secretary/Treasurer
Duane Dubansky
Assistant Treasurer
Richard Samet
Immediate Past President
Daniel Staffenberg
Chief Executive Officer
Board of Directors
Geri Adler
Susan Adolf
Rabbi David Asher
Rabbi Dennis Beck-Berman
Melanie Binshtok
Zach Brenner
Marvin Daniel
Bill Dinkin
Karen Fine
Yael Hutcher
David Galperin
Richard D. Gary
Steve Gillespie
Gary Goldberg
Howard Goldfine
Jill Goldfine
Matthew Grossman
Robin Jackson
Russ Jennings
Barbara Kikner
Rabbi Michael Knopf
Rabbi Yossel Kranz
Roger Loria
Rabbi Scott M. Nagel
Amy Nisenson
Ashley Noell
Joshua Peck
Adam Plotkin
Michael Plotkin
Josh Rubinstein
Elise Scherr
Rabbi Hal Schevitz
Lynn Schwartz
Nathan Shor
Daniel M. Siegel
Michael E. Sievers
Andrew Vosenberg
Elliott Warsoff
Franklin Wolf
Cheri Yochelson
Rabbi Ahuva Zaches
Executive Committee
cont-

February 28, 2018

Christonya Brown, History and Social Science Coordinator
Office of Humanities and Early Childhood
Virginia Department of Education
James Monroe Building
101 N. 14th Street
Richmond, VA 23219

Dear Ms. Brown,

This year, at our request, the Institute for Curriculum Services reviewed materials that have been submitted for consideration by the state in the 2018 History and Social Science Textbooks and Instructional Materials Adoption. They have made recommendations, which we endorse, to correct errors and misleading information regarding Judaism and Jewish history.

The Jewish Community Relations Committee of the Jewish Community Federation of Richmond, the Community Relations Council of the United Jewish Federation of Tidewater, and the Jewish Community Relations Council of Greater Washington (serving Northern Virginia) appreciate the longstanding and fruitful relationship we have enjoyed with the Department of Education. As Jewish community relations organizations and Federations serving Virginia, we appreciate the rigorous review process you have put in place to ensure that our state adopts high quality instructional materials for our children. We welcome the opportunity to comment and do so in a spirit of partnership. As supporters of strong public schools, we want the very best for Virginia K-12 students so they have all the tools they need to succeed as good citizens of our state, country, and world.

The Institute for Curriculum Services (ICS), our partner, is a national initiative dedicated to promoting accurate instructional materials and instruction on Jews, Judaism, and Israel for K-12 students and works in partnership with Jewish organizations, publishers, and educators in Virginia and around the country. Its team employs a scholarly approach, applying a wealth of content knowledge and expertise in teaching, research, and curriculum mapping to its work.

The reviews address quality, accuracy, and balance. We believe that the Institute for Curriculum Services' recommended changes should be made in the interest of historical accuracy and consistency for the sake of Virginia's teachers and students. Students rely on the body of knowledge presented in classrooms to help them reason, problem solve, communicate, and navigate the information they will face in the future. We kindly request that the errors addressed in the attached reviews be corrected prior to the final disposition of the state adoption.
The reviews will arrive as attachments in several emails submitted to textbookcomment@doe.virginia.gov.

We know ICS looks forward to working with all of the publishers to make appropriate edits to the texts. We also ask that if and when issues are identified and corrected in textbooks, conforming edits are made to the corresponding ancillary materials so that students will not be presented with contradictory information.

The Harry & Jeanette Weinberg Campus · 5403 Monument Avenue · P.O. Box 17128 · Richmond, VA 23226
Phone (804) 288-0045 · FAX (804) 282-7507 · www.jewishrichmond.org

APPENDIX

ICS is also sending these reviews to the publishers as we all believe that, by and large, publishers share our goal of producing accurate and balanced instructional materials. In particular, we would like to thank Pearson and McGraw-Hill for the many improvements made to their textbooks based on earlier ICS recommendations. These have resulted in more accurate learning resources for Virginia students.

Thank you very much for your time, consideration, and dedication to ensuring high quality and accurate instructional materials during the final deliberations about materials considered for Virginia's 2018 Textbooks and Instructional Materials History and Social Science Adoption.

Yours sincerely,

Daniel E. Fogel, Director
Jewish Community Relations Committee (JCRC), Jewish Community Federation of Richmond

Miriam Davidow, Chair
JCRC Education Sub-Committee, Jewish Community Federation of Richmond

Robin Mancoll, Director,
Community Relations Council, United Jewish Federation of Tidewater

Steve Adleberg, Director of Education Outreach
Jewish Community Relations Council of Greater Washington

SUMMARY OF VIAB'S ENABLING STATE OF VIRGINIA LAW REMOVING ITSELF OUT OF THE GOVERNOR'S OFFICE

2018 Session
HB 1297 Virginia-Israel Advisory Board; reorganizes as Virginia-Israel Advisory Authority.
Introduced by: Timothy D. Hugo

SUMMARY AS PASSED:

Virginia-Israel Advisory Board; transfer to legislative branch. Transfers the Virginia-Israel Advisory Board (the Board) from the executive branch to the legislative branch. The bill also changes the membership of the Board by increasing the number of citizen appointments by the Speaker of the House of Delegates from six to 10 and the number of citizen appointments by the Senate Committee on Rules from six to 10 and by decreasing the number of appointments of the Governor from 13 to five.

The Joint Rules Committee appoints the executive director to the Board. Funding for the costs of expenses of the members and the operations of the Board, including staffing needs, are made from such funds as appropriated by the General Assembly.

The Virginia-Israel Advisory Board is currently an advisory board in the executive branch of government staffed by the Office of the Governor.[189]

---

[189] HB 1297 Virginia-Israel Advisory Board; reorganizes as Virginia-Israel Advisory Authority, 2018 legislative session, passed
https://lis.virginia.gov/cgi-bin/legp604.exe?181+sum+HB1297

FULL TEXT OF VIAB'S ENABLING STATE OF VIRGINIA LAW PASSED MARCH 30, 2018

CHAPTER 697
An Act to amend the Code of Virginia by adding in Title 30 a chapter numbered 42.1, consisting of sections numbered 30-281.1 and 30-281.2, and to repeal Article 11 (§ 2.2-2424 et seq.) of Chapter 24 of Title 2.2 of the Code of Virginia, relating to the Virginia-Israel Advisory Board; report.
[H 1297]
Approved March 30, 2018
Be it enacted by the General Assembly of Virginia:
1. That the Code of Virginia is amended by adding in Title 30 a chapter numbered 42.1, consisting of sections numbered 30-281.1 and 30-281.2, as follows:
CHAPTER 42.1.
VIRGINIA-ISRAEL ADVISORY BOARD.
§ 30-281.1. Virginia-Israel Advisory Board; purpose; membership; terms; compensation and expenses; staff; chairman's executive summary.
A. The Virginia-Israel Advisory Board (the Board) is established as an advisory board in the legislative branch of state government. The purpose of the Board is to advise the General Assembly on ways to improve economic and cultural links between the Commonwealth and the State of Israel, with a focus on the areas of commerce and trade, art and education, and general government.
B. The Board shall have a total membership of 31 members that shall consist of 29 citizen members and two ex officio members. Members shall be appointed as follows: 10 citizen members appointed by the Speaker of the House of Delegates, who may be members of the House of Delegates or other state or local elected officials; 10 citizen members appointed by the Senate Committee on Rules, who may be members of the Senate or other state or local elected officials; five citizen members appointed by the Governor who represent business, industry, education, the arts, and government; the president, or his designee, of each of the four Jewish Community Federations serving the Richmond, Northern Virginia, Tidewater, and Peninsula regions, each of whom shall be a resident of the Commonwealth; and the Secretary of Commerce and Trade and the Secretary of Education, or their designees, who shall serve as ex officio voting members of the Board.
C. Nonlegislative citizen members shall serve for terms of four years. Legislative members and the Secretary of Commerce and Trade and the Secretary of Education, or their designees, shall serve terms coincident with their terms of office. Vacancies occurring other than by expiration of

a term shall be filled for the unexpired term. Vacancies shall be filled in the same manner as the original appointments. Any member may be reappointed for successive terms.

D. The members of the Board shall elect a chairman and vice-chairman annually from among its membership. The Board shall meet at such times as it deems appropriate or on call of the chairman. A majority of the Board shall constitute a quorum.

E. Members shall receive no compensation for their services. However, all members shall be reimbursed for all reasonable and necessary expenses incurred in the performance of their duties as provided in §§ 2.2-2813 and 2.2-2825.

F. The Joint Rules Committee shall appoint an executive director to the Board. Funding for the costs of expenses of the members and the operations of the Board, including staffing needs, shall be from such funds as appropriated by the General Assembly.

G. The chairman of the Board shall submit to the Governor and the General Assembly an annual executive summary of the interim activity and work of the Board no later than the first day of each regular session of the General Assembly. The executive summary shall be submitted as provided in the procedures of the Division of Legislative Automated Systems for the processing of legislative documents and reports and shall be posted on the General Assembly's website.

§ 30-281.2. Powers and duties of the Board.

A. The Board shall have the power and duty to:

1. Undertake studies and gather information and data in order to accomplish its purposes as set forth in § 30-281.1, and to formulate and present its recommendations to the Governor and the General Assembly;

2. Apply for, accept, and expend gifts, grants, or donations from public, quasi-public, or private sources, including any matching funds as may be designated in the appropriation act, to enable it to better carry out its purposes;

3. Report annually its findings and recommendations to the Governor and the General Assembly. The Board may make interim reports to the Governor and the General Assembly as it deems advisable; and

4. Account annually on its fiscal activities, including any matching funds received or expended by the Board.

B. In addition, the Board shall meet with the Governor at least annually to (i) provide a review of the Board's economic and cultural development activity and (ii) assist in planning an economic development and cultural exchange mission to Israel.

2. That Article 11 (§ 2.2-2424 et seq.) of Chapter 24 of Title 2.2 of the Code of Virginia is repealed.

3. That any unexpended balances of the Virginia-Israel Advisory Board as of June 30, 2018, that have accrued in the executive department pursuant to a general appropriation act shall be transferred to the Virginia-Israel Advisory Board in the legislative department.

4. That the provisions of this act shall not affect current members of the Virginia-Israel Advisory Board whose terms have not expired as of July 1, 2018. However, beginning July 1, 2018, with the exception of appointments to fill the remainder of an unexpired term, the Governor shall not appoint any citizen members to the Board until such time as the number of gubernatorial citizen appointees serving on the Board is less than five.

FAILED SUBSTITUTE BILL THAT WOULD HAVE MERGED VIAB INTO THE VIRGINIA ECONOMIC DEVELOPMENT PARTNERSHIP FEBRUARY 28, 2018

HOUSE BILL NO. 1297
AMENDMENT IN THE NATURE OF A SUBSTITUTE
(Proposed by the Senate Committee on Rules
on February 28, 2018)
(Patron Prior to Substitute--Delegate Hugo)
A BILL to amend and reenact § 2.2-2424 of the Code of Virginia, relating to staffing of the Virginia-Israel Advisory Board.
Be it enacted by the General Assembly of Virginia:

1. That § 2.2-2424 of the Code of Virginia is amended and reenacted as follows:

§ 2.2-2424. Virginia-Israel Advisory Board; purpose; membership; terms; compensation and expenses; staff; chairman's executive summary.

A. The Virginia-Israel Advisory Board (the Board) is established as an advisory board, within the meaning of § 2.2-2100, in the executive branch of state government. The purpose of the Board shall be to advise the Governor on ways to improve economic and cultural links between the Commonwealth and the State of Israel, with a focus on the areas of commerce and trade, art and education, and general government.

B. The Board shall consist of 31 members that include 29 citizen members and two ex officio members as follows: six citizen members appointed by the Speaker of the House of Delegates, who may be members of the House of Delegates or other state or local elected officials; six citizen members appointed by the Senate Committee on Rules, who may be members of the Senate or other state or local elected officials; 13 members appointed by the Governor who represent business, industry, education, the arts, and government; the president, or his designee, of each of the four Jewish Community Federations serving the Richmond, Northern Virginia, Tidewater and Peninsula regions; and the Secretary of Commerce and Trade and the Secretary of Education, or their designees, who shall serve as ex officio voting members of the Board.

C. Nonlegislative citizen members appointed by the Governor shall serve for terms of four years and nonlegislative citizen members appointed by the Senate Committee on Rules and the Speaker of the House of Delegates shall serve for terms of two years. Legislative members and the Secretaries of Commerce and Trade, and Education, or their designees, shall serve terms coincident with their terms of office. Vacancies occurring other than by expiration of a term shall be filled for the unexpired term. Vacancies shall be filled in the same manner as the original appointments. Any member may be reappointed for successive terms.

D. The members of the Board shall elect a chairman and vice-chairman annually from among its membership. The Board shall meet at such times as it deems appropriate or on call of the chairman. A majority of the members of the Board shall constitute a quorum.

E. Members shall receive no compensation for their services. However, all members shall be reimbursed for all reasonable and necessary expenses incurred in the performance of their duties as provided in §§ 2.2-2813 and 2.2-2825. Funding for the costs of the expenses of the members shall be provided by the Office of the Governor.

F. The Office of the Governor Virginia Economic Development Partnership Authority shall serve as staff to the Board and shall designate an executive director to the Board from existing Authority staff.

G. The chairman of the Board shall submit to the Governor and the General Assembly an annual executive summary of the interim activity and work of the Board no later than the first day of each regular session of the General Assembly. The executive summary shall be submitted as provided in the procedures of the Division of Legislative Automated Systems for the processing of legislative documents and reports and shall be posted on the General Assembly's website.

TOBACCO COMMISSION LETTER FORGIVING $210,000 OWED BY VIAB VICE CHAIRMAN CHARLES LESSIN

The Honorable Terry G. Kilgore
Chairman

The Honorable Frank M. Ruff
Vice Chairman

701 E. Franklin Street, Suite 501
Richmond, Virginia 23219

804-225-2027 [Phone]
1-877-807-1086 [Toll Free]
804-786-3210 [Fax]
www.tic.virginia.gov

TOBACCO REGION REVITALIZATION COMMISSION

August 5, 2019

Mr. Charles Lessin
6500 Patterson Avenue
Richmond, VA 23226

**Re: Tobacco Regional Opportunity Fund Performance Agreement
Dated 08/4/14 among the Virginia Tobacco Region Revitalization Commission,
Russell County IDA and Appalachian Biofuels, LLC. (#2941)**

Dear Mr. Lessin,

In 2014, a grant from the Tobacco Region Revitalization Commission (TRRC) Tobacco Region Opportunity Fund (TROF) was provided to your company, Appalachian Biofuels LLC (the "Company") to manufacture biodiesel in Russell County, Virginia (project # 2941). The TROF grant in the amount of $565,000 was provided prior to performance based upon the promise of 40 new jobs. The promised capital investment was $3,500,000. The period of performance was for 3 years from June 30, 2014 – June 30, 2017. The grant was disbursed in two installments, $210,000 in September 2014 and $355,000 in December 2014. The first installment of $210,000 was invested in project-related costs and the second installment of $355,000 was reserved in an escrow account.

In 2016, the Commission was notified that the project was not moving forward due to a drastic decline in world oil prices. In early 2017 the Commission notified the Company that the full grant amount of $565,000 must be repaid for failing to meet the performance obligations. In early January 2018, the Commission's Executive Committee considered an appeal from the Company to reduce the clawback amount. After consideration, the Executive Committee declined to reduce the clawback and requested that the Company work with TRRC staff to develop a repayment plan. On January 22, 2018 the Company repaid the $355,000 leaving $210,000 to be repaid to the Commission.

150

APPENDIX

In a February 2018 meeting with between TRRC staff and yourself, it was agreed that in your capacity as a member of the Virginia Israel Advisory Board, over a two-year period, you would work to meet the performance metrics promised as part of project 2941 (40 new jobs, capital investment of $3.5M) to the Commission's footprint.

In July 2019, at the request of TRRC staff you provided a detailed confidential listing of the projects you have (and continue to be) involved with that are within the Commission footprint. After reviewing the locations, capital investment and jobs provided with these projects, TRRC staff can confirm that you have fully met the employment and capital investment obligations as agreed and the project can be closed. Thank you for your partnership with the Commission and please be in touch should you have any follow up questions.

Sincerely,

Evan Feldman
Executive Director

CC: File
       Russell County IDA c/o Ernest McFaddin

151

TOBACCO COMMISSION REDACTED LIST OF VIAB'S PROJECT PIPELINE SUBMITTED BY VIAB VICE CHAIRMAN CHARLES LESSIN [190]

CONFIDENTIAL   7/22/19

Chuck Lessin
Recent contributions to the Commonwealth of Virginia

Company	Location	Project	Cap Ex	Jobs	Announce
Oran Safety Glass	Greensville County	Factory Expansion	$6.5 million	55	Finalized
			$30.4 million	29	
			$52.2 million	178	
			.75 million	15 (Permanent)	
			$25 million	30 (10 months)	
			$20 million	30 (10 months)	
			$45 million	50 (10 months)	
			$100 million	70 (10 months)	
			$100 million	70 (10 months)	
			$100 million	70 (10 months)	
			$90 million	60 (10 months)	
			$45 million	40 (10 months)	
			$25 million	30 (10 months)	

TOTAL CAP EX: $639.85 million

TOTAL JOBS: 727 jobs

CONFIDENTIAL

---

[190] The Tobacco Commission redacted all of the company names from this list except OSG before release.

SUN TRIBE SOLAR OFFERS ASSISTANCE FOR KING WILLIAMS COUNTY TO RESPOND TO "LOCAL POLITICAL FEEDBACK"

KW King William (county)
Public Schools

David White <dwhite@kwcps.k12.va.us>

E Hunt Project Update- King William Co.

Alex Gregory <alex.gregory@suntribesolar.com>   Mon, Sep 30, 2019 at 5:21 PM
To: David White <dwhite@kwcps.k12.va.us>
Cc: Anthony Stone <astone@kwcps.k12.va.us>, Rich Allevi <Rich@suntribesolar.com>

Dr. White -

I'm reaching out today to provide a quick update on the E Hunt Solar Project.

First off, I want to mention that my management group is putting together a response to the email you forwarded over last week regarding some local political feedback you have received. Like you said it seems with an election coming up everybody likes to try and find a way to get people riled up. I should have that to you tomorrow.

In recent project news, we have run our temporary site access plan through our safety department and everybody is on board. I had my civil contractor update pricing and include the access road in his scope. Thanks again to Tony for helping identify that option of attack.

Currently, we are on track to wrap up permitting on Monday 11/11 with construction mobilization directly following our permit in-hand date. We have finalized the racking and electrical designs with KW co. and everybody is on board with our proposal.

I will be providing an updated project schedule with next week's update as well as details on our preconstruction meeting and mobilization timelines. Feel free to reach out with any specific questions or requests I can help with.

Additionally, I have attached the PowerPoint presentation I gave to the school board if that is of any value. Thanks again for the opportunity to present to the group and don't hesitate to forward any similar opportunities moving forward.

Thanks,

Alexander Gregory

Project Manager

Sun Tribe   Sun Tribe Solar

300 E Main St. Suite 200, Charlottesville, VA 22902

M 919.824.7741 T 800.214.4579 F 434.245.4904

alex.gregory@suntribesolar.com | www.suntribesolar.com

INDEX

ABOUT THE AUTHOR

Grant F. Smith lives in Washington, DC where he researches and writes about U.S. Middle East policy formulation. Smith is director of the nonprofit Institute for Research: Middle Eastern Policy (IRmep).

In his thirty-year professional career as a researcher, Smith has investigated financial services and global telecommunications industries, worked in twenty-two countries assessing the impact of regulatory and trade regime changes and managed multi-country research teams. Smith has a BA in International Relations from the University of Minnesota and MIM (Master of International Management) from the University of St. Thomas in St. Paul. Smith's first research experience examining lobbying took place in the late 1980s as a member of a Minnesota Citizen's League committee investigating public entities that used a significant percentage of their taxpayer-funded allocations to lobby elected officials for ever-larger appropriations.[191]

In 2014, Smith sued the Department of Defense in federal court and won release of a detailed report, contracted in 1987, about the advanced state of Israel's nuclear weapons program. *The Nation* wrote about it in the article "It's Official: The Pentagon Finally Admitted That Israel Has Nuclear Weapons, Too." In 2015, Smith sued the Central Intelligence Agency and won release of 131 pages of formerly classified information revealing its overseas agents obtained compelling evidence that Israel stole U.S. government-owned weapons-grade uranium in the 1960s to build its first atom bombs. The CIA's refusal to share this information thwarted two FBI investigations into the diversion. It is the subject of continuing Freedom of Information Act litigation as estimated toxic site cleanup costs approach half a billion dollars.

Smith's essays about the lobby are frequently published at the Antiwar.com news website and the *Washington Report on Middle East Affairs* magazine. This book is Smith's ninth about the Israel lobby. IRmep is co-sponsor of the annual conference about Israel, the Israel lobby, Palestine, elections and free speech at the National Press Club. It has become a gathering point for a broad range of intellectuals, activists, reporters and educators determined to expose and defeat the institutionalized corruption driving deadly and wasteful U.S. Middle East policy formulation.

---

[191] "Because That's Where the Money Is: Why the Public Sector Lobbies" Citizens League Report, June 28, 1990

www.ingramcontent.com/pod-product-compliance
Lightning Source LLC
Chambersburg PA
CBHW022335280326
41934CB00006B/649